Learn How to Study

Learn How to Study

– a Realistic Approach

DEREK ROWNTREE

Professor of Educational Development
at the Open University

timewarner
paperbacks

A *Time Warner* Paperback

© Derek Rowntree 1970, 1976, 1988, 1998

First published in Great Britain in 1970 by Macdonald and Co.
(Publishers) Ltd, London & Sydney
Reprinted in 1972, 1973, 1974
Second edition 1976
Reprinted 1978, 1980, 1983, 1984
Third edition 1988
Reprinted 1989, 1990
Reprinted by Warner Books 1993
Reprinted 1993, 1995, 1997
Fourth (redesigned) edition 1998
Reprinted 1999, 2001
Reprinted by *Time Warner* Paperbacks in 2002

Rowntree, Derek, 1936–
Learn how to study. – New ed.
1. Study techniques – Manuals
I. Title
371.3'028'12

ISBN 0 7515 2088 8

Typeset in Plantin by M Rules
Printed in England by
Polestar Wheatons Ltd., Exeter.

Time Warner Paperbacks
An imprint of
Time Warner Books UK
Brettenham House
Lancaster Place
London WC2E 7EN
www.TimeWarnerBooks.co.uk

Contents

For Mark and Leo

About this book

Please read this FIRST

> 'They tell you all sorts of things about study skills –
> usually the things they've found useful themselves,
> twenty years ago – but I don't know how much of it
> seems applicable . . . in the end it's up to you to sort out
> your own best way, isn't it?'
>
> Third-year student

This book will *not* tell you how to study. That's why it's not called *How to Study*. The fact is, I can't tell you how you should study. Nor can anyone else.

There is no one best way of studying. A method that suits me may not suit you. You yourself may well use different methods when studying different topics or with different purposes in mind. Furthermore, the methods that suit you this year may be different from those that suited you last year. And by next year you may need yet more new methods.

Why learn to study?

So why have I bothered to write this book at all? And why should you bother to read it? Simply because all of us need to *learn* how to study. It is not an ability we are born with, like the ability to breathe.

True, we are born with the ability to learn. We do it every day of our lives, usually without even being aware of it. But studying is a rather special form of learning. We usually do it with some specific purpose in mind. It also involves the expectations that other people have of us. We usually don't improve at it unless we give some thought both to our own purposes and to those other people's expectations.

If you are to do the best you can as a student, you need to understand what you want out of studying and what learning means to you – as well as developing some appropriate study skills. (Appropriate, that is, to the different kinds of study situations in which you find yourself, both now and later in your life.) This book aims to help you think realistically about some key aspects of studying, and so help you learn what might be best for you.

The reflective student

Learning to study is essentially a do-it-yourself operation. You'll get ideas from this book. You'll get even more from teachers and fellow-students. But, in the end, it's up to you. You need to be able to *reflect* on your own experience of studying and decide what changes of approach might best suit you. Throughout this book, and afterwards, I hope to get you asking yourself:

- What are my present approaches to studying?

- Which of them am I satisfied with?

- Which of them am I less than satisfied with?

- How can I find out about other approaches I might consider trying?

- Which, having tried them, seem to be improvements on my existing approaches (at least for some purposes)?

- Are there yet other approaches I might usefully try out, and adapt to suit my special needs?

This questioning approach, once you get used to it, should be yours for life. The need for 'lifelong learning' is now widely accepted. All of us – to keep up with change and/or stay employable – are going to be studying, off and on, formally or informally, throughout our working years, if not beyond.

In my own work, the inrush of new technology over the last few years has meant I've had a lot to learn about ways of using computers in education. This has forced me to find many new answers to the questions I posed above and I see no end to the process. Becoming a professor does *not* mean you have finally cracked the study problem once and for all!

Terminology

This book is written for students of all kinds. You may be studying in an educational setting – sixth form, college or university. You may be studying in a training context – taking part in training or staff development provided by your employer. You may be studying chiefly at home in your spare time. To save repetition, I shall use the word 'college' to stand for whatever body is responsible for your course (whether it is a college, university, employer or whatever). Similarly, I shall use the word 'campus' to stand for the site on which that 'college' is located.

If, like most student, you are studying on campus, you may be taking courses that are based around lectures and classroom work or you may be taking a flexible, open or resource-based learning course in which you learn chiefly from specially prepared materials. If you are studying at home you may well be working on a 'distance learning' course. I shall use the term 'materials-based learning' to cover both distance learning and on-campus courses based on learning from materials (see Chapter 8 for more details). And I shall use the word 'tutor' to stand for lecturer, teacher, instructor and so on.

How I'd advise tackling this book

Unless you're in a hurry to read a specific chapter for some reason of your own, I *strongly suggest* you start with Chapters 1, 2 and 3, in that order. Much of what follows in later chapters will be echoing the issues I raise in those first three. After Chapter 3, it's up to you. I think the subsequent chapters follow a fairly logical sequence – and I would particularly recommend you read Chapter 5 before Chapter 6 – but you won't miss any vital connections if you choose to read Chapters 4–11 in whatever order best suits your interests.

In any case, I doubt if you'll find that one read-through is enough. Students tell me that this is the kind of book they need to come back to from time to time. Some of the suggestions I discuss may, on first reading, seem merely interesting. But later, as new study problems become urgent, you may want to return to those suggestions to see if some of them can now help you find practical solutions.

Questions and activities

Just one more thing. This book is not an ordinary 'straight read' with page after page of continuous prose. From time to time, you'll see a blue line across the page like the one below. What is this for?

Well, it means I have asked you to do something that gets you to think about what I've said. This will usually be a question (like 'What is this for?' above) or some sort of activity, like ticking appropriate boxes in a questionnaire. Occasionally I will ask you to write a sentence of your own, so you may want to keep a notebook by you. These questions or activities are meant to aid your learning.

Below the ruled line, I go on to give my comments on the activity you have just completed. That's what I've just been doing in the paragraph above. So, whenever you see a blue line like the one above, it means:

'Please pause here and complete this activity before you go on to read my comments.'

If you were just to read straight on without trying the question or activity, you would often be unable to make much sense of what followed – and you certainly wouldn't gain as much as you otherwise might from the book.

You will also notice that each chapter ends with a set of 'Follow-up activities'. These suggest ways in which you might want to apply what you are reading in this book to the real situation in which you are studying.

In particular they encourage you to make the most of your fellow students, and learn from one another's experiences of learning. This may not be so easy if you are a part-time student or are doing a course by distance learning. But even distance learners usually have a chance to meet occasionally or to exchange ideas via telephone, fax, email or computer networks. In fact, it was in my work with distance learning that I first saw the value of student 'self-help groups' and realised how they might benefit on-campus students also.

1
The myths and realities of being a student

> *'Some days I feel really right about being here – I've just said something perceptive in a tutorial or I've got an essay back with some good remarks. Other days I feel a real phoney and think I must have scraped in by some fluke of the system. Days like that, I look around the room and everybody seems far brighter than I am, and superbly organized and just . . . well, effortless superiority they call it, don't they? I sometimes wonder if I basically haven't got what it takes, and how long will it be before they rumble me.'*
>
> First-year student

Doubts and uncertainties

One's early days as a student are often full of uncertainties and self-doubts. You are taking on a new role in a new social set-up. It's different in so many ways from what you've known before. And where do you fit in? With whom do you compare yourself? Just who do you think you are?

If you've recently come from school, you may be disconcerted to find yourself no longer one of the high-fliers but, in this more select company, merely average. And if you've come as a mature student, after years in a full-time job, you may feel amazed by the relative naïvety of your younger colleagues – yet perturbed by what appears to be their relative confidence as learners and what you suspect may be their greater powers of concentration and memory. If you are a 'distance learning' student, studying on your own for most of the time, you may feel completely in the dark as to how you compare with other students taking your course.

Obviously, we come across people who make us think about our weaknesses. And, in so doing, it is all too easy to overlook our strengths. But the fact is, you almost certainly wouldn't be in college unless you've got what it takes. Whether you can make the best of whatever it is you've got depends on whether you can keep your nerve and build on your strengths.

The myth of the super-student

Self-doubt often sets in because we compare ourselves with an idealized image of what we think the perfect student ought to be like – and consequently judge ourselves lacking. New 'distance learning' students, like those in the Open University, are particularly prone to this – because it may be some weeks before they meet other students and learn that they share the same doubts and anxieties as themselves.

For example, consider the following features which students have mentioned to me when asked to describe the ideal student. Tick the first box if you feel that feature is *essential* to being the sort of student you'd like to be. Tick the second if you feel you *could* learn to be like that (or are like that already).

Essential *Could you?*

1 They are superbly organized for studying and they are so self-disciplined they never lose concentration or get sidetracked ☐ ☐

2 They ruthlessly ignore family, friends and social life ☐ ☐

3 They read every book and article on the reading list ☐ ☐

4 They take in the sense of everything they read, quickly and without effort ☐ ☐

5 They remember everything they've read and everything they've heard in lectures ☐ ☐

6 They take masses of well-structured notes and have impressive card index systems ☐ ☐

7 They speak fluently, confidently and knowledgeably at seminars and tutorials ☐ ☐

8 They can zip off a first-class essay on any topic at a
single sitting ☐ ☐

9 They are always supremely confident about how well   ·
they are doing in their studies ☐ ☐

10 They never get anxious about examinations and always
achieve excellent exam results ☐ ☐

---

*What did you think of the 'ideal student'? How essential did you think the
points mentioned were? And how did you feel about yourself in comparison? Let's check through them:*

1 Organization and concentration
Of course, it helps to have some kind of timetable for your studies.
Otherwise your life will be full of muddle, unpleasant surprises and
missed deadlines. But who can be so self-disciplined that they never lose
concentration or get sidetracked? Students obsessional enough to aim at
such single-minded determination are liable to be incapable of changing
their plans. They may thus be unable to cope effectively with new
demands (or opportunities) that crop up unexpectedly.

2 Family, friends and social life
Again, this sounds obsessional and inflexible. You are not just a student
but also a human being, living and working among others. Learning to get
on with them is just as important as learning from books and lectures. For
many students (often quite successful ones) the social life is the most
important aspect of being at college. As one student put it:

> *'My priority is all my clubs and societies. I'm not saying
> I'm not interested in the academic side . . . it's a
> question of balance. But if that was my sole interest, well,
> I think I might just as well be doing an Open University
> course.'*

Besides, even if you are concentrating on your academic work, you can
get invaluable moral support from family and friends. Indeed you can get
unexpected insights into your work while chatting with people who have
no special knowledge of your subject – they so often ask such tricky
questions!

3 Reading everything

Trying to read everything on most college reading lists is a recipe for disaster. Most contain far more material than any single student is expected to get through. The name of the game is *selectivity*. How can you find out which items in the list (or parts of items) are truly relevant to *your purposes* in studying? The important thing is to attain a deep understanding of a careful selection – not to get a hurried and superficial familiarity with more than you need. As one student commented:

> *'I felt perpetually guilty until I realized I didn't have to read everything. Now I'm enjoying it. It's stopped being a chore. I even feel free to read other things I've found for myself.'*

4 Effortless understanding

Don't believe it. Students who reckon to be taking in ideas quickly and effortlessly are either deluding themselves or are reading material they are already familiar with. Getting a grasp on new ideas is never that easy. After all, they so often have to replace some old ones that you're already quite comfortable with. Learning doesn't have to be painful, but no amount of study technique is going to make it effortless.

5 Total recall

There are two mistakes in this notion. First, no one can possibly remember everything they've read or heard. Second, and more importantly, college-level learning is not about remembering but about *understanding*. I would ask not whether students can remember what they've read or heard but whether they have made sense of it. What has it meant to them? Can they make use of it?

6 Masses of notes

Who needs masses of notes? There is no point in trying to produce your own hand-written version of a book or lecture. The amount of notes you make should depend on your purpose in making them. But they should have some kind of sensible structure, or they'll be too difficult to make sense of when (if?) you come back to read them again. As for card indexes, or even personal computer databases, constructing them and looking after them too often takes up time that might be better spent on learning something.

7 Fluent public speaking

It is worth making the most of group situations to try out your ideas on tutors and other students; their reactions may help you learn. But there is no need to feel abashed if you are not as fluent as you would like to be. Students who seem to shine in tutorials and seminars are not always those who do well in writing or practical work.

8 Quick, effortless essay writing

Another myth. Writing is never that easy. Even a three or four hour sitting may not be enough to allow for the kind of drafting and redrafting that most of us need to go through to produce an essay we feel satisfied with.

9 Supreme confidence

'Students who keep their heads when all about are losing theirs' (to misquote Kipling), are probably somewhat out of touch with reality. Even the best of students has anxieties and self-doubts from time to time. The real test is whether you can admit them to yourself, be clear about their cause, and seek to cope with them by taking action and/or by talking them over with tutors and other students.

10 Examination excellence

Well, perhaps there are some students who don't get anxious about examinations; perhaps some even look forward to them. But they aren't necessarily the ones who turn in the excellent results. A certain amount of stress is unavoidable for most of us, and may even be necessary if we are to get sufficiently psyched up to give of our best.

The secrets of success

To sum up then, the features suggested for the 'ideal student' are either unattainable or of questionable relevance in the real world of studying. So I hope you didn't set your heart on attaining too many of them. They are not features that will help you succeed as a student.

What, then, do you need to succeed? Three things:

1   You need a sense of *purpose*. Why are you studying? What do you hope to get out of it – both out of your course as a whole and out of each individual session of studying?

2 You need to understand the *situation* within which you are studying. In particular, you need to know what *you* can expect from other people (especially tutors) and what *they* expect in return.

3 You need to develop the *strategies* to satisfy their requirements while at the same time getting what you want out of the learning situation.

Let me give you a crude example. Some students enter college with no purpose other than to fill time – and hopefully pick up some sort of ticket to a job at the end of it. But they soon find that the college staff will expel them unless they show they are learning whatever the staff regard as being worthwhile. So, they must acquire whatever strategies are necessary to satisfy the college staff that they are entitled to stay on and collect their ticket.

Many students, needless to say, have loftier motives in coming to college. But they are often equally blind to what is expected of them and how to meet those expectations.

Put the other way round, there are three reasons why students fail to do as well as they might. Rank the three items in the list below from 1–3 according to which you feel to be most (1) and least (3) true of you.

- They are unclear as to what they want ☐
- They are unclear as to what is wanted from them ☐
- They are unable or unwilling to provide what is wanted ☐

Whatever your answer, this book should help on all three counts. And if you feel totally self-confident about all three aspects, check back on my comments about 'supreme confidence' above!

Chapters 2 and 3 are meant to get you thinking about your purposes in studying and the demands being made on you. Chapter 4 is about getting organized to meet those demands. And the remaining chapters should get you into the habit of reviewing the strategies and skills you will need in learning, and trying out new approaches where this seems worthwhile.

> **The most important 'study technique' is that of believing in your ability to learn.**

Follow-up activities

1   Think of the many activities that are involved in being a student – e.g. those mentioned on pages 6–7 . Which three do you feel you do (a) most competently and (b) least competently at present.

2   Consider the things you feel you do least competently. Do you feel you do them competently enough to cope with the demands likely to be made on you? If not, can you see any ways of improving at them?

3   Discuss with other students what they see as their strengths and weaknesses. What leads them to feel the way they do? Can you see ways of learning from one another?

2
Studying and learning

> 'I never really thought about what studying was or what learning was. I mean, I'd had years of it at school and now I was going to have a few more years in college. Like being on a conveyor belt, really – you're too busy rolling along and keeping on top of things to worry what it's all about. Pity really, to think what I could have made of my chances if I'd been more clued up.'

That's a comment from a not untypical student looking back on three years of college life. She got her degree and went straight into the sort of career she'd been hoping for. And yet she sounds regretful. Like many students, she realized too late that she'd missed something.

Thinking about studying and learning

Many students, some successful and some not, miss out because they never stop to think about studying and learning. For them, studying and learning never become objects of their attention in the same way as, say, chemistry or computing do. Since they don't reflect on their experience of studying and learning, they don't learn as much as they should about them. (So they probably don't learn as much about chemistry or computing as they might, either.)

In this chapter, I want to mention a few aspects of studying and learning which you may or may not have thought about before. Above all, I want to encourage you to get into the habit of thinking and also talking about such matters. That way, you'll learn not just from your own experience but also from the experience of your fellow-students. To begin with:

Why are you studying?

How did you come to be a student? Different students have different reasons. I myself became a student in order to be a student – student life was what I was after. The actual subject to be studied was very much a secondary concern. In fact I'd left it so late applying that the only course on which I could get a place committed me to three years of the subject I'd liked least among my specialisms at school. But no matter, I was in. Once in, I eventually developed other reasons for studying, but that's enough of me for the moment.

Purposes in studying

What about you? You may be just starting as a student. You may be well into your course. You may be approaching the end of your studies. But what do you feel are your main *purposes* in studying?

The clearer you are as to what you want from your studying, the clearer you can be as to how you might best set about it. There are many approaches to study. Not all of them will be suited to your purposes. Without giving thought to what you want from study, you may find yourself locked into inappropriate approaches.

Here are some reasons or purposes mentioned to me by a number of students when asked why they were studying. Which of them are closest to the way you feel about being a student? Pick, say, the *three* closest and rank them 1 to 3 in the boxes alongside.

A *'I've always been keen on this subject and I've always wanted to spend as much time as possible on it. Now I can do that. Great!'* ☐

B *'This was the area I was best at in school, and it just seemed natural to go on and get myself a degree in it. I mean, why not?'* ☐

C *'I'm studying this course because it's directly relevant to the sort of work I'll be doing. I can already see how to apply most of the new stuff I'm learning, and I know it will help me do the job better and enjoy it more.'* ☐

D *'If I get through this course I'll have no trouble getting the sort of job I want. The college has a really good record of placing people, and fortunately the employers aren't too bothered about grades – so long as you pass.'* ☐

E *'To be honest, I felt my mind was stagnating. I want to broaden my horizons and become a bit better able to think about what's going on in the world . . . to be a bit more mentally alive, really.'* ☐

F *'I want to prove myself to other people. My teachers didn't reckon me, and nor did my parents – and even my husband's a bit sceptical. But if I can get a degree, well, that'll show them, won't it?'* ☐

G *'What I'm mainly interested in is the social life. You can't go wrong in a place like this if you want a good time, and the sports facilities are fantastic too.'* ☐

H *'I'm mixing with a lot of people and learning ways of dealing with them – sort of personal politics! And I think a lot of the contacts I'm making will be useful to me later.'* ☐

Clearly, the reasons listed above are just a few of the many that might be given for studying. Ask some of your friends, and you'll no doubt get a totally different set.

Differences in purpose

However, I think we can see some rather important differences among the reasons listed above. To begin with, reasons G and H are not really reasons for studying at all. They simply indicate what the people were getting out of being at college. Such students may be doing nothing more than the minimum necessary to survive their courses. Their purposes are largely *social*.

Academic vs vocational vs personal purpose

Look at A and B, by contrast, and we can see people with an *academic* purpose. Both of these students are following an interest or ability in a particular subject. Students C and D have *vocational* purposes. They are interested chiefly either in performing well in a job (C) or in qualifying for a job (D). Students E and F have what we might call a *personal* purpose. Student E is looking for some kind of mental development. Student F is out to prove herself, and show other people they were wrong about her.

You may or may not have found difficulty in deciding what your main purpose is. You may certainly have more than one type of purpose in mind, and they may be somewhat mixed together. Perhaps your purposes vary from one area of your studies to another. Also, you may start out with one sort of purpose, but develop others as you go along. For instance, it's not uncommon for students to start at college intending simply to qualify for a job or a promotion (vocational) – only to find themselves getting lit up by the subject they are studying (academic).

Appropriateness of purpose

No one purpose is necessarily better than another. But you can ask yourself how *appropriate* your purposes are. This depends what your long-term aims are and what your college is demanding from you as a student. For example, suppose you hope to go into an occupation for which some high-grade qualification is essential. Then you may not get what you want if your purposes are purely social and/or personal (unless you are absolutely brilliant). Again, suppose your course is very much aimed at developing vocational abilities, e.g. as a computer technician or a teacher. You might feel rather uncomfortable if you had academic purposes that made you much more interested in the theoretical rather than the practical aspects of the subject.

In general, it is better to have more than one purpose in studying. The more reasons you can find for doing what you have to do, the more energy you're likely to put into it – and the more you are likely to get out of it. Students who remain open to the unexpected will often find themselves getting more out of a course than they bargained for, e.g.

> '*I mean, I did two years of this subject at school and I though I'd just be doing more of the same. But, you know, deeper and more stretching sort of thing . . . But what we've been doing, like projects and relating it to our own lives, well, it's opened my eyes to a whole lot of things I never even expected to think about. It's altered the way I look at everything, really. I'm a different person. I don't know whether I'm any more employable though [laughs].*'

So, your purposes in studying are liable to affect the way you study and how you feel about what you are doing.

There is another important difference in purpose that may influence what you do. Each of the four purposes can be tackled in at least two different ways:

Look back at the boxes you picked out against the eight reasons quoted above. Were most of your three boxes against.

reasons A, C, E and G ☐

or reasons B, D, F and H? ☐

Intrinsic vs extrinsic purpose

If you went for A, C, E and G then you chose what we might call intrinsic *purposes. That is, in A, C and E, studying the course is its own reward. (Forget G and H, for the moment, because they aren't really to do with studying at all.) With A, C and E, the enjoyment of the subject, or the increase in job competence or the personal growth is an end in itself.*

With B, D, F and H, however, the reward is *extrinsic* to the course. Studying is merely a means to an end. Your true purpose is to demonstrate academic attainment (B), to qualify for a job (D) or to impress somebody else by doing well on the course (F).

So, as well as having academic, vocational or personal purposes in studying, you may also have intrinsic or extrinsic ones. 'So what?' you may ask. Simply this: you'll probably find you can apply yourself more readily to studying – especially when the going gets tough – if you choose courses that offer you *intrinsic* satisfaction. That way, you'll be working for what *you* can get out of the course – not simply to prove things to someone else.

What, on the other hand, if your motivation is extrinsic? Then you'll be liable to:

● resent much of the work you do on the course ☐

● do as little as you can get away with ☐

- tackle things in a routine, superficial way ☐

- miss out on aspects of the course that might have been intrinsically satisfying ☐

- have difficulty getting down to work ☐

- get tired and bored easily ☐

- gain very little of lasting value ☐

- judge your progress only by grades and the opinions of your tutors rather than by how you think and feel about what you have learned ☐

Tick any of the above problems you believe you have already.

Don't worry if you occasionally have such feelings about some parts of your work. For various reasons, it is not always possible to find intrinsic satisfaction in all parts of everything one has to do at college. I've heard many students of, say, economics or education complaining about being made to take a course in statistics. They don't see its relevance. I remember being such a student myself. Sometimes, the best one can do is find parts of the subject that are of intrinsic interest and hope that they'll make one feel at least a little bit more enthusiastic about the rest.

On the other hand, there can be dangers in following only one's intrinsic purposes. There may be plenty of scope for intrinsic satisfaction in the course, but your tutors may be making demands that require you to study for extrinsic reasons also. In other words, you won't always be able to satisfy them just by satisfying yourself. Consider, for instance, the remarks of this student (taking a degree in Economics, Law and Accountancy):

> *'My absorbing interest has always been economics. I've read all around the subject and I've done far more work than is set for the assignments. And my marks have always been first class. But I've still got to keep up in law and accountancy, and I suppose I just about get by with a lot of help from my friends on assignments and that, but I don't bother with many lectures.'*

As it turned out, this student didn't do enough to satisfy his law and accountancy tutors and eventually had to give up the whole degree course.

So, the moral is: seek out the parts of your course that are intrinsically satisfying – whether academically, vocationally or personally; but don't overlook or neglect the parts that just have to be done for extrinsic reasons.

What do you mean by learning?

Studying is about learning. If we're talking about learning how to study, then we're talking about learning how to learn. But what do you mean by learning?

I have asked a number of students this simple question. It often gives them quite a bit of trouble. Partly this is because the word 'learning' can be both:

a) a verb – as in learning accountancy or metallurgy

b) a noun – indicating the results of (a), i.e. what the learner has learned

That is, learning is a *process* (a) that leads to a *product* (b).

Students' views

When they talk about the process of learning (a), some students use 'learning' to indicate the same kinds of activity they think of as 'studying'. Thus, one said, 'Reading mainly, and listening to lectures, doing practical work, all that kind of thing.' Such students are commenting only on the externals – what we can *see* of the learner's actions. So I would then ask a further question: 'OK, so what is going on in your mind while you are reading, listening or whatever?' I'll pick up this point about the 'internals' of learning later.

When they talk about learning as a product, students reveal very different ideas about what they expect to result from the process of learning. Some find it difficult to conceive of results or a product at all – other than passing an examination or getting praised by a tutor.

What do you mean by 'learning'? What might *you* be referring to if you said, 'I really learned a lot from that course'? Write a sentence in your notebook beginning 'Learning is . . .'.

Here are the remarks of some other students. Put a tick or a cross in two of the boxes to indicate which is most (✓) and which is least (✗) like your idea of learning.

A *'Being able to remember as much as possible of what I have been studying – all the names, dates, places, etc.'* ☐

B *'Knowing all the essential facts and theories and so on, and which ones are relevant to particular questions.'* ☐

C *'Understanding what lies behind all the ideas and approaches you've been working on and how they all hang together.'* ☐

D *'Being able to relate what I've been studying to my own life so that I see a different significance in things.'* ☐

E *'Being able to combine what you've done on the course with your other experience and apply it in quite new ways.'* ☐

F *'Feeling you're a bigger and better (wiser?) sort of person because even when you've forgotten the details, you know you've somehow increased your capacity for life.'* ☐

G *'Your learning is who you are; you realize you are learning all the time you are living.'* ☐

Did you find it easy to agree or disagree strongly with any of the above statements? You may have found it difficult to see the difference between one or two of them. I did myself. But I think we do have seven rather different viewpoints here. They raise a number of interesting talking points and should help you to think some more about your own views of learning.

The simple and the complex

I have arranged the above students' statements in what I see as a progression. The progression goes from a simple view of learning to more and more complex ones.

Learning as memorizing

Students A and B both see learning in terms of *memory*. Student A is not too choosy; he'd like to remember everything he's studied. He sounds as if he'd like his head to contain the entire contents of the books he's read and the lectures he's listened to. Why he should want such learning is not clear from the quote.

Student B is perhaps slightly more sophisticated or at least more selective. She wants to remember only the essential facts. And she does seem to recognize that learning may include an ability to make some judgement as to their relevance in particular situations.

Both of these students would probably see the process of learning as being chiefly a matter of memorizing. Theirs is perhaps a *University Challenge* or *Mastermind* idea of learning – the well-stuffed brainbox ready to spill out correct answers in response to unambiguous questions. They might, for example, have no trouble with a question like 'How did Hemingway end his novel *A Farewell to Arms*?' Yet they might feel less comfortable with one like 'If you had been Hemingway's editor, what kind of case would you have made for preferring one of the other four endings Hemingway considered for that book?' (Unless, of course, they had already had an opportunity to memorize an acceptable answer.)

Learning as understanding

Students C and D might be happier with the latter kind of question. They have moved beyond memorization. They seem to be concerned with *understanding* and with *meaning*. Student C is interested not just in learning and remembering the 'ideas and approaches' she's been working on. She realizes that something 'lies behind' them and she wants to understand what it is. She is looking for patterns and relationships that help make sense of it all. Student D clearly expects what he is learning to be related to the real world (his 'own life'). And he too is looking for new meaning (or 'significance') in the real world as a result.

Learning for application

You may not see a lot of difference between students D and E. But I would suggest that student E does make clear one new aspect. He explicitly states that his idea of learning involves the capacity to relate new ideas to his existing ideas and apply them in 'quite new ways' – presumably ways that were not explored on the course. Presumably, also, they would be ways that were unique to him since no other student would be relating the new ideas to the same stock of existing experience as he is. Clearly, both D and E are talking about *applying* (and even building on) the ideas they have studied – not about remembering those ideas as they first met them.

Learning for personal development

Student F and G also have a lot in common in their notion of learning. Both expect to be changed as people by the experience of learning. Student F suggests that even when the detail is forgotten, something will remain that makes him, in some way, a wiser and more capable person. Student G goes perhaps even further by offering her view that a person's learning *is* the person – and that this enables her to see her life as a learning experience.

Looking back over these seven students, I would pick out four clearly different conceptions of learning. Tick the one you feel is *most important* to success in the kind of course you are studying.

1 Memory of facts that have been studied ☐

2 Understanding the meaning of what has been studied ☐

3 Ability to apply one's understanding to new problems ☐

4 Becoming a more aware and more competent person, not simply in those subjects one has studied ☐

Understanding is paramount

I expect you will have ticked 2 or 3 – broadly in line with the notions of students C, D, E and F. Memorization is not likely to be of key importance at your level. College courses are not usually concerned with facts that have to be committed to memory. They are more likely to be concerned with ideas – concepts, principles, approaches and theories – that have to be understood.

As for 4 (personal development), college staff often speak approvingly of it, but it is not usually assessed and is not usually essential in satisfying the course requirements. Fortunately, many students achieve such personal development while in pursuit of 2 and 3 – and, of course, through their outside activities in sports, publications, drama and music, or whatever.

Grappling with new ideas

So your most pressing concern in learning will probably be to take on board a whole lot of unfamiliar ideas. This is not always easy – especially when those new ideas involve *new ways of looking at the world*. After all, we've each got our own ways of looking at the world already. We are often quite comfortable with our viewpoints and approaches. We may resist having these cosy ideas challenged by new ones.

I first remember this happening to me, long ago, when I was learning to speak French. It seemed to me obvious that this meant having a thought (in English, of course) and replacing the English words with the corresponding French ones. But after I'd been learning for a while, some teacher tried to tell me that word-for-word translation won't work – and that one needs, in effect, to think French thoughts in order to speak French. This idea seemed too far-fetched to take on board at first. I did my best to ignore it, struggling to carry on as well as I could with the approach I was already familiar with. Only after some time – in which I met not only French people who found my efforts amusing but also increasingly complex material that my approach seemed incapable of dealing with – did I gradually abandon my old ways and grow into the new (and more powerful) way of looking at communication between people from different backgrounds.

Overcoming learning barriers

I mention such learning difficulties in order to remind you that the course of true learning does not always run smoothly. Don't be disheartened if you sometimes run up against what seem like barriers in tackling a new idea or approach. Don't dismiss it out of hand or tell yourself you'll never understand it. Think of all the similarly difficult or awkward ideas you've met in the past and are now quite comfortable with.

The way to make sense of new ideas or approaches is to apply them to whatever situations or problems they are supposed to help with. Your memory of them will usually develop as a *by-product* of such repeated attempts to apply them and, in the process, refine them and make them your own. You will not remember them merely by trying to fix a mental snapshot of them in your brain.

What do you do when you're learning?

What is going on in your mind while you are learning? What, if anything, are you looking for? What do you think you are doing? How do you know when you've finished doing it? What do you think you've got out of it? It probably won't surprise you to hear that different students give very different answers to questions like these – even when they all appear to be doing the same thing, e.g. reading the same book.

For many years now, psychologists, sociologists and educationalists have been researching into how students set about learning. They've come up with a number of findings that can help a student see her or his own practices in a new light. (I've given references to some of this research in the Bibliography at the back of this book.) Naturally, I've written this book with these findings in mind. Right now, however, I'd like to draw your attention to a few particular findings that may help you consider:

1 Do I have a customary approach to learning?

2 What alternative approaches are there?

3 Might an alternative approach sometimes be more appropriate to my purpose?

Surface- vs deep-level approaches

This is a very useful, basic distinction. Surface-level learning is the approach taken by students who concentrate on *words* while deep-level learning concentrates on *meaning*.*

I'll illustrate this with quotes from some students who were asked how they set about reading a particular article. See if I've already said enough for you to be able to tick them off as taking a surface-level (S) or deep-level (D) approach.

	S	D
A 'I tried to pick out all the main facts.'	☐	☐
B 'I was trying to work out what the author's assumptions were.'	☐	☐

* See Marton *et al.* in 'References'

	S	D
C 'What was the main point of the article, what was it really getting at.'	☐	☐
D 'Anything that stood out as a fact or piece of information – names, figures, that sort of thing – I tried to memorize it.'	☐	☐
E 'What sort of questions can they ask me, that's what I was thinking . . . so I just tried to get it all into my head.'	☐	☐
F 'I was trying to work out whether the author's ideas tied in with my experience.'	☐	☐

The students taking a surface-level approach were A, D and E. Those taking a deep-level approach were B, C and F.

Basically, the surface readers were looking at the words on paper, trying to memorize anything they thought they might be tested on or might need to reproduce. Their ideal might have been to be able to read back the words from a kind of photograph in their heads.

The deep readers, on the other hand, were looking through and beyond the actual words. They were looking for meaning – for what the author's intentions were, for what he was getting at, for the extent to which his ideas made sense. Their ideal might have been to explain this meaning, even perhaps criticize it, in their own words.

Can you change levels?

Some students may tend to use a surface approach as a matter of routine. Others may approach everything in a deep way. This will reflect what they want to get out of learning – the 'products' we discussed earlier in this chapter.

But most students are probably able to take either a surface or a deep approach, depending on the circumstances. You have probably taken a deep approach when you felt you needed to *understand* something, and a surface approach when you felt that all you had to do was *remember* it.

Even students who normally take a deep approach will sometimes go for the surface. If, for example, they find something impossible to understand, they may resort to trying to memorize it instead. Again, if students feel they are going to be tested in a way that concentrates on facts (e.g. by multiple-choice questions), they may decide that the surface approach is the appropriate one.

It has also been noticed that students who are anxious and uncertain about what is expected of them, or who are pressed for time, are liable to take a surface approach. The unfortunate thing, however, is that this approach often seems to defeat its own purpose. If you haven't understood something, you are less likely to remember it. So, the deep approach, if you can relax enough to go for it, is likely not only to make the subject more interesting (because you understand it) but also more memorable.

Levels in all learning

By the way, this deep-surface difference doesn't just occur in learning from books. The same thing can happen in learning from other media.

For example, consider learning from lectures. Can you think of a lecture where you've been involved in a deep way and one where you've been involved in a surface way? Do you think you took the most appropriate approach in each case? Why?

If, for example, your lecturer was presenting an interpretation or a line of argument, then you'd probably need a deep approach in order to make sure you grasped the sense of it all. If, on the other hand, you were already familiar with the meaning of your lecturer's theme and she or he was merely presenting data which you were clearly expected to memorize, then you might be safe in taking a more surface approach. But you'd be even safer if you later thought in a deep way about how the examples related to the general theme. This would probably make the subject more interesting and help you recall the details for far longer.

Serialist vs holist learning

This is another distinction pointed out by researchers.* Some learning strategies have been called 'serialist' and others 'holist' (i.e. whole-ist).

If students adopt a serialist strategy to a topic, they work through it step by step – aiming to master each sub-topic thoroughly before considering

* See G. Pask and B.C.E. Scott, 'Learning Strategies and Individual Competence' in *International Journal of Man-Machine Studies*, 4, 1972, pp. 217–53

any other. Their focus is narrow and they try to steer a straight and clear line through the subject matter. If you ask them later about what they have been studying, they will usually tell you about it, sub-topic by sub-topic, in the same order in which they studied them.

Students adopting a holist strategy, on the other hand, prefer to get some sort of feel for the *whole* topic before they look in detail at any of its component parts. They like to roam freely over the topic, examining it from many viewpoints, looking at interesting examples or for connections with what they already know. They seek some sort of broad (if shallow) understanding of what the topic as a whole is about before they commit themselves to trying to understand its detail.

What about you? Would you say you:

● prefer to take a *serialist* approach? ☐

● prefer to take a *holist* approach? ☐

● vary in approach according to topic? ☐

Some researchers think students tend to be locked into one approach or the other, regardless of topic – almost as an aspect of their personalities. Others think that students can vary their approach according to the situation. Perhaps you can think of different topics in your own studies that might lead you to take the two different approaches?

As you may imagine, neither approach is necessarily better than the other. There is certainly no tie-up with surface and deep approaches. Serialists and holists are equally likely to be seeking understanding and meaning, rather than mere remembering. They would differ simply in whether they were trying to understand from the parts to the whole or from the whole to the parts. Though some learning tasks, and some teaching, may encourage the serialist approach and some the holist, a combination of the two may sometimes be needed for a full understanding.

Possible dangers

If you feel you tend towards serialist learning, you need to beware of failing to grasp the total picture. You may be so busy with the bits and pieces that you never see the broad themes and general principles that run across them all. You may be even less likely to see how the topic as a whole relates to other whole topics. Your understanding may be fragmented and difficult to build upon.

If, on the other hand, you tend towards the holist approach, you run the risk of over-generalizing about a topic or jumping to conclusions on the basis of insufficient evidence. You may over-simplify some of the broad themes and general principles. You may fail to grasp important distinctions and exceptions to the general rules because you have paid insufficient attention to understanding details.

Knowing about these two contrasting sets of risks may help you to keep your strategy flexible enough to avoid them both.

Syllbs vs Syllfs

Here is a third way of identifying two very different approaches to learning.* Are you a Syllb or a Syllf? (Or, as is often the case with these twofold distinctions, sometimes one, sometimes the other?) Let's try to find out.

Consider what your preference would be if you were *forced to choose* one or other option on each of the following aspects of studying. Put your tick in either box A or box B accordingly.

		A	B
1	(a) to be told exactly what subjects I am supposed to be studying, *or*	☐	
	(b) to decide for myself what subjects to study		☐
2	(a) to study subjects where everything is cut-and-dried and my personal opinion will not be relevant, *or*	☐	
	(b) to study subjects in which experts do not always agree about issues and where my personal opinions will be relevant		☐
3	(a) to study the same topics within a subject as everyone else, *or*	☐	
	(b) to be free to choose a different set of topics from other people		☐

* See Hudson in 'References'

	A	B

4 (a) to study my topics in the same sequence as everyone else, *or* ☐ (A)
(b) to be able to study them in whatever sequence most appeals to me ☐ (B)

5 (a) to have a set amount of time for studying each topic, *or* ☐ (A)
(b) to be able to decide how much time I spend on each topic ☐ (B)

6 (a) to be told exactly what knowledge and abilities I am expected to acquire as a result of the course, *or* ☐ (A)
(b) to be able to decide for myself what knowledge and abilities I want to acquire ☐ (B)

7 (a) to be taught by tutors who are expert in transmitting their own knowledge of the subject to students, *or* ☐ (A)
(b) to be taught by tutors who are expert in helping students develop their own interests in the subject ☐ (B)

8 (a) to be given one or more books containing all the material I was supposed to master, *or* ☐ (A)
(b) to be encouraged to go out and learn from whatever sources I found most useful ☐ (B)

9 (a) if tests are given, to have no choice as to which questions I must tackle, *or* ☐ (A)
(b) if tests are given, to have a wide choice of questions ☐ (B)

If you put nearly all your ticks in the A column, then you are most likely what the researchers call a 'Syllb'. If nearly all your ticks are in the B column, then you are most likely a 'Syllf'. If your ticks are fairly evenly divided, then there's perhaps a bit of both in you.

Syllbs are students who are 'syllabus-bound'. Basically, they feel more comfortable if they know exactly what is expected of them. They want to know exactly what they have to do to achieve recognition from people like tutors and prospective employers, who will be rewarding their efforts.

Syllfs, on the other hand, are 'syllabus-free'. They prefer to go their own way, enjoying as much freedom as possible to decide what they will learn, how they will learn it, and how they will be assessed. They are likely to believe that their personal viewpoints are an important aspect of learning. For them the most satisfying rewards are those that come from feeling that one has progressed towards one's own goals.

What best suits your situation?

As always with these twofold distinctions, there is no best way to be. It all depends. Perhaps you'd like to think about whether your preferences suit the study situation in which you find yourself. Are they appropriate? For instance, if you are something of a Syllf, I could imagine you feeling very restricted by some science-based courses I know of. Similarly, if you are more of a Syllb, you might feel uncomfortable on courses with an extensive project or dissertation where students are expected to explore a subject of their own choice with little or no direct teaching.

Can one be a Syllb in some situations and a Syllf in others? Can one adapt to meet the demands of different courses? Can one's preferences change as one gains in experience and/or self-confidence? What do you think? Anyway, next time you come to choosing courses, you may want to examine them in terms of the features mentioned in the list above. Which courses are most likely to suit *your* preferences?

Activists, theorists, pragmatists and reflectors

By now you may be tired of twofold distinctions between approaches to learning. You may even be thinking that researchers into student learning fall into two categories – those who believe students can be divided into two categories and those who don't! So let's finish this chapter with a couple of perspectives on types of learning that have more than two categories.

Do you tend to be an activist or a theorist, a pragmatist or a reflector? Two researchers* have developed a questionnaire that can help you find out – on the basis of whether you agree or disagree with 80 statements such as these:

- I often 'throw caution to the winds'.

- Quiet, thoughtful people tend to make me uneasy.

- I like to relate my actions to a general principle.

* See Honey & Mumford in 'References'

- I steer clear of subjective or ambiguous topics.

- I am careful not to jump to conclusions too quickly.

- On balance I do the listening rather than the talking.

- What matters most is whether something works in practice.

- Most times I believe the end justifies the means.

Your answers enable them to suggest the strength of your preference for each of the four styles they identify. Few people are likely to favour one style to the exclusion of all others. But it is common for one to predominate, with the others being used less often or not at all. None of the styles is always superior to the others. All may serve you well in different contexts.

Styles	respond WELL to, e.g.	respond POORLY to, e.g.
Activists *'Here, let me do that.'*	New problems, being thrown in at the deep end, team work . . .	Passive learning, solitary work, theory, precise instructions . . .
Theorists *'Yes, but how do you justify it?'*	Interesting concepts, structured situations, opportunities to question and probe . . .	Lack of apparent context or purpose, ambiguity and uncertainty, doubts about validity . . .
Pragmatists *'So long as it works.'*	Relevance to real problems, immediate chance to try things out, experts they can emulate . . .	Abstract theory, lack of practice or clear guidelines, no obvious benefit from learning . . .
Reflectors *'I need time to consider that.'*	Thinking things through, painstaking research, detached observation . . .	Being forced into the lime-light, acting without planning, time pressures . . .

Does any one of the above sound most like you, sometimes or most of the time? Does this set of categories help you see what sort of teaching you might prefer?

I've mentioned these categories because it may help you see what a challenge tutors face in teaching in a way that suits all students. The teaching would, for instance, need to be:

- novel and participatory enough for the Activists

- intellectually rigorous enough for the Theorists

- practical enough for the Pragmatists

- leisurely enough for the Reflectors.

It is a rare teacher who can manage all this at the same time. That's why, if your tutors don't often match your preferred style, you might need to think about finding *other ways* of learning in the way you prefer and/or becoming more *flexible* in your styles. I hope this book will help you in this.

How relativistic are you?

Finally, let's consider a perspective that looks at how students' views of learning may develop over the months and years.

Suppose your tutor tells you that tomorrow your group will be having a lecture from a distinguished outside expert, Dr Fox. She will be discussing with you *four* different theories which have been put forward to account for a particular phenomenon that you are studying at present. Which of the following reactions to this news would you *most* agree with?

  A 'If there are four different theories floating around, then I suppose we ought to have heard of them all. So long as she tells us which is the right one, to make sure we don't waste time learning the others.' ☐

  B 'Good teachers often present you with more than one answer to give you practice in working out which theory is correct. It's something you have to be able to do on your own. But I hope she doesn't make the right theory too difficult to spot.' ☐

C 'Presumably she'll be telling us about all four theories
because they all have some value in explaining the
phenomenon. I expect we'll be hearing about the assumptions
behind each one, what sort of scope each has, its strong
points and shortcomings, and so on.'   ☐

*This question arises out of research into how students' ideas of 'truth'
are likely to develop over time. The researcher* actually identified nine
stages of development, but the three chief ones are illustrated above.*

Stage A above shows a student who thinks in terms of right/wrong or
good/bad. In every subject, the student believes there are 'right' answers
and these are known to the experts. It is the responsibility of the experts
to teach these right answers to students.

In stage B above, the student has similar general beliefs about knowledge (right/wrong answers) but recognizes that there may be some
uncertainty as to which is the right answer. The experts may engage students in working out which is the right answer and/or may require them
to learn more than one.

In stage C, the student has come to see knowledge as *relativistic*.
Different answers may be right because they can all be justified in their
different ways. So several answers may be worth knowing about. This is
not because we can't yet be sure which of them is 'right', but because they
are all more or less helpful in explaining or shedding light on the phenomenon in question – a poem, an historical controversy or even a
sub-atomic event in physics. So the student will be interested to hear how
Dr Fox analyses the four theories in terms of what they assume about the
phenomenon, how much of it each accounts for, how well each fits with
the known data, and so on. (At the same time, the student will also be
conscious that even 'expertness' is relative. Other equally respected
experts might present a different case for the four theories, or even present a different set of theories.)

Clearly the three students suggested here will all go to Dr Fox's lecture
with very different *expectations*. So they are all likely to get something very
different out of it. Who has got out of it what the course demands? We
cannot tell without knowing more about the context.

* See Perry in 'References'

1 **Can you think of parts of your own subject in which relativistic thinking is more appropriate than a right/wrong attitude?**

2 **How comfortable are you with such relativistic thinking?**

Alternative viewpoints

1 *Most subjects, even those that are science-based, have areas in which there are no right/wrong answers but simply different interpretations or models, each with more or less to contribute to one's understanding of some problem.*

2 *Many students have difficulty in coming to terms with a relativistic view of knowledge. They feel adrift in a sea of uncertainty. It may be some while before they feel confident enough to say where they stand among the competing theories and interpretations – to commit themselves to a reasonably consistent view of things, while admitting the validity of viewpoints that conflict with theirs.*

Anyway, I hope you'll feel comfortable with the relativistic approach to studying I've taken in this book. You won't find any lists of right and wrong ways to study – just a variety of different practices, each of which may have its virtues for different individuals in different situations.

Making your own knowledge

In fact, this is a very fitting theme on which to end this chapter. For what, after all, is learning to study? It is not a matter of learning a set of study skills that will improve your ability to get a load of knowledge into your head. Knowledge is not a commodity to be picked up ready-made, as if from a supermarket shelf. Instead, you need to be involved in the *making* of your knowledge.

If you are to understand and make sense of a subject, the knowledge you gain will be different from that gained by other students on the same course. Not only will the knowledge be in you, but there will also be something of you in the knowledge. So learning how to study in higher education is basically a matter of getting wiser about learning and under-standing.

Thus, to the extent your situation allows it, you will be able to set aside any lingering notions of learning as the memorization of true facts.

Instead, you will learn to apply approaches that will enable you to understand a diversity of viewpoints and commit yourself to those that make most sense in terms of your own considered experience.

This getting of wisdom may take some time, and may often make your head ache. But it's what will remain with you long after you've forgotten what you've studied in college. It's how to learn about life. It's the key to lifelong learning.

You can learn from studying how other students learn. But, even in the 'same' situation, no two students will learn the same things – nor will they learn in the same ways.

Follow-up activities

1 Try to pick out some fellow-students who might be interested in talking about studying and learning.

2 Find out from other students what they think of as 'learning'. Discuss with them some of the ideas in this chapter.

3 Show the quotations on page 19 to some of your colleagues and discuss with them the idea of academic/vocational/personal and intrinsic/extrinsic approaches to study, and which are most likely to be encouraged in your department.

4 Think back to some recent learning experience that you felt bad about and to one that you felt good about. Jot down some notes about what made the one bad and the other good. If possible, compare notes with a colleague and see if you can agree on any factors that make for satisfying or unsatisfying learning.

5 Find out from other students (especially in subjects other than your own) the extent to which they are looking for 'right answers' or are willing to work with alternative viewpoints.

6 Think of an idea or issue within your subject that you found difficult or uncomfortable at first but do so no longer. Try to make some notes to account for why you found it difficult or uncomfortable at first and why you do not find it so now. Does this tell you anything about how you might tackle ideas or issues that you may be having problems with now or in the future?

3

Understanding your situation

'What did I hope for when I came here? Maybe some sort
of real academic collaboration between teachers and
students, and an air of intellectual debate. I think I
expected some sort of "broadening of the mind" –
different anyhow from the grubbing after facts we did at
school – but you eventually realize that what the lecturers
want is to be left alone (most of them, anyway) and just
get us to serve them up with all the same old stuff
they've been dishing out to us all term. The emphasis is
all on grades, not on learning. I'm really disenchanted
with the place . . . I can't wait to finish.'

Learning does not take place in a vacuum. You are studying in a particular situation – a particular college, a particular department, a particular subject group. Many students give little conscious thought to their situation once they've overcome any initial surprise or uncertainty. They just start taking it all for granted. They make no effort to understand the situation or consider how they might best survive and prosper within it.

Different situations have different things to offer you – and make different demands on you in return. What happens if you don't understand your situation? You may find yourself blindly adopting approaches to studying that really don't suit you – and perhaps nursing unexplained resentments. Alternatively, you may fail to develop approaches that are essential to getting what you want out of your time in college.

Being able to stand back and look at one's situation, as if with the eyes of an outsider, is an ability well worth acquiring. It will put you in a better position to make decisions and take action – not just as a student but in any organization or community within which you may be working in the future. It enables you to be realistic.

You can set about analysing and understanding your situation from many viewpoints. And you are likely to find it more fruitful if you can do it in collaboration with fellow-students who share that situation with you. In this chapter, we'll consider just three aspects of your situation:

1 The social climate

2 The learning climate

3 The assessment system

Obviously each of these is closely related to the other two.

The social climate

Colleges differ from one another in many ways. So do faculties, departments and subject areas within any one college. Even one year-group of students may differ quite markedly from others. One way in which they may differ is in what we may call the 'social climate'. That is, how do members of, say, your department or subject-group relate to one another? How does it feel to be a member of the group?

For instance, how would you feel about the following statements, which are based on students' comments about their various departments or subject areas? Tick SA, A, D or SD according to whether you would Strongly Agree, Agree, Disagree or Strongly Disagree with each statement as a description of your department.

	SA	A	D	SD
1 Special efforts were made to help new members joining the department and it is easy to feel you belong in it	☐	☐	☐	☐
2 The staff are mostly approachable and helpful, and there is little or no feeling of 'them and us'	☐	☐	☐	☐
3 Students are treated as individuals rather than as numbers on a register	☐	☐	☐	☐
4 The administration is human rather than bureaucratic	☐	☐	☐	☐

5 There are adequate facilities for students to meet and chat informally ☐ ☐ ☐ ☐

6 The atmosphere among students is friendly and collaborative (rather than distant and competitive) ☐ ☐ ☐ ☐

7 Staff clearly take into account that students have other things to concern them in addition to their studies ☐ ☐ ☐ ☐

8 Each student has a personal tutor to help with problems ☐ ☐ ☐ ☐

9 The personal tutor is both easily available and helpful ☐ ☐ ☐ ☐

10 The general atmosphere is warm and friendly ☐ ☐ ☐ ☐

I doubt if all your ticks are in the SA column, but I hope you've got more ticks under SA and A than under D and SD.

Departments differ greatly, as you will know if you have dealings with more than one, or if you compare notes with students elsewhere. The department in my first university consisted, as I remember it, of a *place* – a couple of corridors where we students went to check the notice-boards and make appointments with staff who were scarcely ever there. Yet other departments I've known since are memorable not as places but as *communities* – staff and students in regular and congenial contact.

The initiation

The tone is often set by the way new students are introduced into the department. One student told me:

> 'My initiation was like being welcomed into prison. The head of department hectored us for half an hour about all the things we could and couldn't do. All the penalties that might befall us. How tough things were going to be. How if we failed it would be our fault not theirs. And then (perhaps the opposite of prison) he said, "Take a good look at the person

*sitting either side of you; the chances are that one of you
won't still be here at the end of the course." We couldn't
decide whether that meant a drop-out of one third or a half,
but it wasn't exactly an upbeat start.'*

Other departments take a different approach to motivating their new
entrants. At one initiation I observed, all the department staff were present, as well as some second-year students. The head of department gave
a friendly talk, cleverly laced with anecdotes calculated to recognize and
yet allay students' anxieties. She concentrated on the opportunities for
students to grapple with new ideas and find new strengths and convic-
tions in themselves rather than harping on about departmental
regulations and demands. The students then split up into small groups,
each with a member of staff and a second-year student, to discuss the
course in more detail. The atmosphere was immediately both intellectual
and welcoming rather than rule-ridden and alienating.

For distance learners, the initiation can be crucial. Unless the system
is one in which they can start with a visit to the campus or local centres,
it will be done at a distance – probably through printed materials. The
students may already be feeling remote and a bit uncertain about what
they might be letting themselves in for. If the materials are not warm and
welcoming, clear in their guidance and reassuring about the things that
might be worrying students, many will drop out before they have started.
A friendly phone call from their tutor, however, might convince them that
the college really does have a human side and cares about them as well as
its own bureaucratic requirements.

Staff–student relations

Such starts usually indicate what is to follow. In some departments, staff
are aloof and indifferent to students.

*'All these guys are interested in is their research. We
students are just the price they have to pay for the privilege
of a cushy life. They know they're here indefinitely. We're
just passing through – we're just the punters.'*

In other departments, staff seem to respect students as junior members of
the same academic 'club'. They share meals and coffee breaks with them,
and even invite them home.

Such behaviour would be talked of as 'pandering' in certain departments, where I've known 'The Students' Friend' used as a term of disdain for a colleague who showed any signs of caring about students' problems. Yet students say: 'Just a nod in the corridor can be enough to make you feel you belong' or 'If he calls you by name, it makes a big difference.'

If your tutors recognize you as a full human being, rather than merely as a learner, then they are more likely to take account of other (non-learning) aspects of your situation that affect your studies. I don't know what these might be in your case, but many students – especially in their first year – find themselves distracted from study by such factors as alcohol, drugs, sex, friendship and family problems, accommodation and, of course, the ever-pressing shortage of cash.

Personal tutors are often able to get to know students personally and give special help. But this doesn't always work out. Sometimes students are reluctant to approach them – 'You really have to psych yourself up,' said one student. Sometimes they find them difficult to get hold of or unhelpful when they do. As one told me:

> '*He hardly looked up from his paperwork. Just told me to make an appointment. I could have been about to commit suicide for all he knew.*'

Staff attitudes naturally have their effect on how students work together as a group. Friendly staff usually encourage friendly and collaborative relationships among students. If staff are cold and distant, students *may* band together ('us *vs.* them') to solve their common problems. Alternatively, they may drift apart and act competitively, even if it's just by kidding one another about how much or how little work they are really doing.

The learning climate

But, despite its importance, the social climate is just the background to studying. In the foreground is the *learning climate*. This depends on the teacher–learner relationship between you and your tutors.

Here are some statements that *might* describe this. Tick the appropriate box according to whether you agree (Yes), disagree (No) or are not sure (?) that each statement is true in your situation.

	Yes	No	?
1 As students, we have a clear picture of the course as a whole – e.g. its aims and the main events that lie ahead	☐	☐	☐
2 The assessment system seems fair and reasonable	☐	☐	☐
3 The tutors mostly seem to be highly expert in their subjects	☐	☐	☐
4 The tutors are not too dogmatic or biased in their views	☐	☐	☐
5 They are willing to discuss alternative viewpoints, even those we put forward	☐	☐	☐
6 They are enthusiastic and interesting in their teaching	☐	☐	☐
7 They seem able to look at their subjects from the viewpoint of the ignorant newcomer as well as that of the expert	☐	☐	☐
8 They take steps to check that we really understand what they are talking about	☐	☐	☐
9 We are not worried about asking them very basic questions that might show them how little we have understood	☐	☐	☐
10 They are prepared to set aside time for helping individuals with learning difficulties	☐	☐	☐
11 The amount of work we have to do is not excessive	☐	☐	☐
12 We are allowed a reasonable amount of independence to decide what and how to learn	☐	☐	☐

I hope you have been able to agree with a fair number of the above statements. I am only too aware that many students cannot.

Seeing the course as a whole

Taking item 1, for example, a vital part of understanding your situation is to have a good grasp of what is involved in your course *as a whole*. Yet students regularly say things like:

> *'Nobody gave us any sort of introduction to the course. We just walked in and, bang . . . straight away we were scribbling notes about a load of formulae.'*

Or

> *'We talk a lot among ourselves about what they might be expecting from us . . . and there's lots of different ideas . . . but no one's really surprised when they announce something unexpected like a three-day field trip in ten days' time. It would have been nice to have more advance notice.'*

In some departments, it can be quite a while before students see the course as a whole. Valuable time can be lost, for example, before students on certain sociology, psychology or medical courses realize that they will not be 'working with people' as much as they had anticipated; or that the 'industrial experience' they had expected from certain engineering courses will be very limited.

Knowing about the course's assessment system (item 2) is an especially important aspect of the whole picture. I'll say more about that later in the chapter.

Tutors' expertise

As for item 3, you want to know that your tutors are reasonably expert but even this can sometimes have its downside. As one student remarked (linking items 3 and 7):

> *'Some of the staff just have no idea how far we are from their level. They're so steeped in the knowledge themselves that they've forgotten what it's like to be ignorant!'*

This is linked too with items 8 and 9. Many students complain, for example, of:

> '. . . lecturers who just sweep in, read from their notes and
> sweep out again, with no attempt to ask us what we make
> of it all. They obviously don't give a toss.'

Yet others will mention, with relief, someone like:

> '. . . this lecturer we have who always breaks us up into
> small groups so that we can discuss the lecture so far
> and agree on questions to ask him about points. Then
> each group puts their question and he usually builds the
> rest of the session around dealing with the answers. You
> really feel you've had some input, and got your problems
> dealt with – and there's no embarrassment.'

Tutors who encourage students to voice their difficulties or uncertainties
in a group situation will probably be equally helpful if approached indi-
vidually (item 10). But it is possible that some who seem reluctant in the
first situation will be helpful in the second. What is your experience? If
there are things you don't understand, and fellow-students can't help
you out with them, can you afford *not* to discuss them with your tutor? Or
would you fear the possible loss of face even more than the effects of
remaining in the dark?

Tutors' personal styles and viewpoints

What students often seem to appreciate in their tutors, even more than
expertise or even the ability to lay down a clear line of argument, is *enthusiasm*. They mention both kinds touched on in item 6 – enthusiasm for
their subject and enthusiasm for finding ways of making it interesting.

> 'If they're enthusiastic, then it's difficult not to get caught
> up in it – especially if they involve you in thinking things
> through or planning a project, and seeing how they operate.
> I can think of two subjects I've done where I'd have had no
> particular interest, basically, except I got these tutors who
> infected me with their own enthusiasm and now I'm really
> keen on those subjects.'

And what about items 4 and 5? It is not uncommon for a department to
build up a staff who have a common ideological commitment. I even met

a professor of geology who told me: 'We are a Marxist department and our students study Marxist geology.' (No, I didn't know there was a Marxist way of studying geology, either.) Your tutors may or may not have such a shared commitment. And, even if they do, they may be quite open to alternative approaches.

On the other hand, even an individual tutor may be unshiftably committed to his or her hobby horse. The essence of 'understanding your situation' here is to find out the nature and strength of your tutors' viewpoints. Then you can decide whether you are able to go along with them or whether you must take whatever risks you can foresee in adopting an alternative viewpoint in the work you produce.

Workload

Workload (item 11) has a considerable influence on the learning climate. Students often complain that too many classes or too much lab work prevents them from doing enough independent reading. They also complain of getting too many essays to write at once, set by different tutors who seem unaware of how much each of them is expecting of students at the same time.

Unfortunately, if you feel under this sort of pressure, your learning is liable to be surface-level and unsatisfying. As one student put it:

> *'I'm a full-time essay writer. I don't have time to really get into one subject before I'm on to the next.'*

Independent learning

Finally, item 12. How much independence your tutors allow you will depend largely on their views about teaching and their subjects. Tutors vary in their views of what *teaching* is all about just as students differ in their views of learning. For example, do they regard students as empty vessels to be filled or flames to be lit? Do they see teaching chiefly as a matter of conveying a fixed body of subject knowledge which all students must take on board and be able to reproduce? Or are they more interested in enabling students to play a part themselves in the construction of their own knowledge? If the latter, they are more likely to get you learning through discussion and maybe even doing some kind of project learning where you work on topics of your own choosing.

Does the learning climate suit you?

Think again about your own purposes in studying, and about your views on what learning is and the approaches you prefer (which we discussed in Chapter 2). To what extent does your local 'learning climate' (as we've examined it above) suit your needs? Do you feel:

- it suits them very well? ☐
- it suits them tolerably well? ☐
- it doesn't suit them at all well? ☐

If your 'learning climate' suits you less than tolerably well, you may be one of the regrettably large number of students who give up their studies every year. If there is any danger of that, do discuss your unease with students and (selected) tutors. If you can't get the climate changed, consider migrating to a more congenial one – that is, to a new course and/or a new department. It usually can be done.

The assessment system

Understanding how your work on a course is assessed is a key element (if not *the* key element) in 'understanding your situation'. Why is this? It is because the assessment system reveals what the course is *really* expecting of you. And this may be rather different from what the college prospectus and head of department's introductory statement say is expected.

Whatever you want from the course, you may not survive long enough to get it unless you make sure you know what the course wants from you. In fact, a close look at some assessment systems might convince you that you wouldn't be able to get what you want from the course anyway.

Questioning your assessment system

Here are some of the questions about your assessment system that you should be able to answer. Tick the box if you already can.

1 How frequently do I have to hand in essays or other assignments? ☐

2 Are all the assignments compulsory? ☐

3 How frequently must I sit examinations? ☐

4 Are all the examinations 'traditional' or are some more 'open' (e.g. questions issued in advance, no time limit)? ☐

5 How much choice of questions or topics do I have on assignments and in examinations? ☐

6 Who will be assessing my work? ☐

7 What criteria will they use in assessing it? ☐

8 How quickly will they tell me the results of each assessment? ☐

9 In what form will I get the results – e.g. pass/fail, a letter grade, a percentage, oral or written comments? ☐

10 Which assignments or examinations will count towards my overall grade or 'result' on the course? ☐

11 Will any other work that is not formally assessed also count – e.g. practicals, contributions to seminars, etc.? ☐

12 Do I have any choice as to which of my work is to count? ☐

13 Will my self-assessment of my work be taken into account? ☐

14 Will there be assessment of group work? ☐

15 In what proportion will each form of assessment (e.g. essays and examinations) contribute to my overall result? ☐

16 If I fail one or more assessments (or courses within a programme) can I still stay in the course and get at least an overall pass? ☐

17 Can I appeal against any of the assessment results and/or ask for reassessment by another assessor and/or have a second try at the assignment or exam? ☐

18 If I have not been able to answer some of the above questions, can I see how to get the necessary information? ☐

Clearly, there is no shortage of questions to ask about the assessment system. Maybe you can think of yet other questions, relating to your particular situation, that I haven't just mentioned.

Where to find out

Perhaps you'd agree that question 18 is one of the most important – where to find information you don't already have. If there are things you need to find out, consider consulting:

- college 'guides to the system'
- department guides
- course guides
- 'alternative' guides (if any) produced by students
- subject tutors
- personal tutor
- fellow-students
- students who've been through the course ahead of you
- assignment topics set for previous students
- copies of past students' assignments (with marks/comments)
- examination papers from previous occasions
- written reports of the examiners (if any)
- and any other likely sources you can think of

Official vs hidden curriculum?

For my money, the most important question in the previous list is question 7 – what *criteria* will your assessors be using? That is, what will they be looking for in your work? What will be well regarded and what will not? For instance, one tutor told me: 'I've got to be sure they know a wide range of basic facts, or they'll have nothing to build on.' Another told me: 'Ideally, I want to encourage in my literature students the capacity and confidence to say something that makes me rethink my own conception of an author or literary work.'

The problem here is that what your tutors are looking for may not always be so obvious as it might seem. What the college/department/ tutors *say* the course will be aiming at – and assessing you on – is *not* always exactly or entirely what does get rewarded in the assessment system. As well as the official curriculum – describing what you're supposed to be learning – there is often a hidden curriculum – whatever it is you are *actually* rewarded for.*

The hidden curriculum is what you have to satisfy in order to survive and prosper in your situation. It may include such qualities as punctuality at classes and speaking with deference to certain tutors. It may include reading a wider range of material than is merely required for the course. It will almost certainly be reflected in what tutors are really looking for in your work.

For instance, many introductory lectures and printed course guides would claim the course is expecting students to develop such qualities as the following:

- 'Sound understanding of the basic concepts of the subject matter and the relationships between them' ☐
- 'Critical thinking' ☐
- 'Independent judgement' ☐
- 'Analytical rigour' ☐
- 'The ability to argue a case convincingly' ☐
- '. . . to engage in collaborative problem-solving' ☐
- '. . . to integrate theory and real–world practice' ☐
- 'The ability to think like a geophysicist/historian/philosopher/pharmacist, etc.' ☐
- 'To become an independent learner' ☐

Which of the above kinds of aim do you think might be echoed by tutors running the course *you* are taking?

Aims like those above are very common and no doubt your course has one or two of them, or something very like them. Too often, however, some of them get lost on the way to the assessment system.

---

* See Snyder in 'References'

Facts *vs* thinking

Part of the problem is that some kinds of ability are easier to assess than others. In particular, it is easier to test factual knowledge (memory) than any of the more important intellectual capacities like 'understanding', 'critical thinking' or the 'ability to argue a case convincingly'.

Researchers have often commented on the results of this. Medical students, for example, who could give you all the evidence in favour of evolution might prove quite incapable of defending the theory in argument with an anti-evolutionist. Students of English literature might be able to give you an impressively rigorous analysis of a poem they had studied before, yet be quite at a loss when presented with one that was unfamiliar to them. Such anomalies usually arise because the supposedly more important qualities and abilities were never assessed – and therefore never learned.

So, it is important to understand what your tutors will *actually* be looking for in assessing your work. And this may be different from what the official aims of the curriculum suggest. If you have regular assignments to tackle, you may get a good idea of what kind of work they will reward – both in assignments and in examinations. As one student told me:

> *'Some of them are just dictating notes at us and that's what they want to hear back from us in the exams. But two I could mention are training us in how to approach the subject and question the way it looks at the world. They want us to develop our own approaches and justify our own conclusions.'*

What do you get asked to do?

To begin with, what sort of assignments do you get set? Do they, for example, ask you to think critically, to analyse complex issues or to argue a case convincingly? Or do they seem chiefly concerned with getting you to draw the facts together and present them coherently in your own words? Do you get asked to apply the methods of a geophysicist, historian, etc. to new evidence or new primary source material? Or are you usually asked to comment on the findings and conclusions of other geophysicists and historians?

How do your tutors respond?

What sort of response do tutors give to your efforts? Do you get encouragement when you show 'independent judgement' and challenge ideas that your tutor holds precious? Or do you get slapped down? And do you get support when you bring in examples from your own experience ('integrating theory with real-world practice')? Or are you told that academic essays are no place for personal anecdotes? Do you feel that you will be rewarded most for getting close to some answer they have already in mind, or rather for coming up with an angle that may even be new to them? Does your grade seem to vary with the amount of factual detail you manage to cram in?

By and large, the way your work is treated (whether it is formally assessed or not) should give you a good idea of what *abilities* tutors are looking for.

Which topics are emphasized?

The topics dealt with on the course are also worth watching – especially if certain topics seem to get more than their fair share of time. They may reveal your tutors' hobby horses. This is why it is useful to know which tutors will be assessing your work. In revising for exams, you may want to pay special attention to their favourite topics. As one professor recalled:

> 'When I was an undergraduate at Cambridge in the mid-1950s, the philosophy dons were split by a deep doctrinal dispute. It became, for the prudent finalist, a matter of working out which faction had the majority on the examining board that year, and then of tailoring one's answers either to fit in with the rather tight, logical and unadventurous demands of the one group, or the looser, more discursive and imaginative expectations of the other.'

How are you affected?

1 Do you feel you already have a good idea of what tutors will be looking for when they are assessing your work?

2 In general, do you feel you have a good grasp of what your assessment system will be demanding of you?

3 Can you see ways in which this knowledge might affect your approach to your studies?

Knowing what the assessment system demands from you is important in two ways. Obviously, it may influence the way you prepare for assignments and examinations. But it may also influence the amount of effort you put into other aspects of the course. If you are reasonably sure that certain activities or topics are not going to count much for assessment purposes, you may decide not to invest too much time and effort in them. This may be especially likely if you don't find them intrinsically satisfying anyway or if you are labouring under a heavy workload. Such a strategy is sometimes glorified with the name of 'selective neglect'.

The list, 'Where to find out', on page 46, gives a broad idea of where to get the information you need. By way of rounding off this chapter, you may be interested to hear about three different approaches that students have been observed to take towards understanding their assessment system.

Cues – the deaf, the conscious and the seekers

Researchers have noticed that students vary in how aware they are of cues or hints given by staff that might help them in performing well in assessment.* Consider the differences between the following:

1 The cue-deaf
These students believe that success in assessment depends on 'working as hard as you can'. There are no tricks of the trade. Staff will set examination questions that ensure a fair coverage of the work you've done. There's no point trying to guess what questions will come up – you've just got to revise everything. And there's no point expecting staff to drop hints about what questions are going to come up, because they won't. And whatever impression you make on staff during class work, it won't affect your assessment results.

2 The cue-conscious
These students believe staff are liable to drop hints that might be useful to them in the exam and they need to keep alert for them. They may get

* See Miller and Parlett in 'References'

cues as to which aspects of the subject staff are particularly interested in, and may even get some cues as to which topics are likely to come up or (equally usefully) not likely to come up. All the same, luck will play a large part in exam success. They believe that the impression they make on staff during seminars and the like will affect their assessment results; but they do not believe there is anything they can do deliberately to create a favourable impression.

3 The cue-seekers
Like the second group, these students believe it is possible to obtain hints or cues that will be useful to them in the examination. They also believe that the impression they create on staff will affect their results in assessment. They differ from the second group, however, in that they actively seek cues and work to create a good impression. Thus, they have as much interaction as possible with staff. They deliberately set about 'making their mark' in class work, for example by regularly asking thoughtful questions or offering examples from their reading or work experience. So the tutor comes to look on them as his or her keen students. They might try to build on this impression in order to develop a sort of friendship. At all events, they will try, whenever they can, to button-hole a tutor over a cup of coffee. This can enable them to get the tutor talking about the subject, disclosing his or her personal interests, and perhaps giving some sort of answer to a question like: 'Is that the sort of thing that's likely to come up on the exam, then?' This group differs from the others in believing that it is *strategy* (not hard work or luck) that makes for success in exams.

Now, these are not watertight categories. They are more like overlapping positions along a scale. You could lie somewhere between 1 and 2 or between 2 and 3. In fact, you might respond differently in different courses. Nevertheless:

(a) Which one of these approaches is *most* like yours?

(b) Which of these approaches do you think is likely to get the *best* assessment results?

(c) Which is likely to get the *poorest* assessment results?

In the original research, the best assessment results generally went to the cue-seekers and the poorest to the cue-deaf, with the cue-conscious scoring somewhere in between. How far these results are due to their attitudes to cues is difficult to say. It is even more difficult to be sure that becoming more cue-conscious or cue-seeking would make a difference for you in your situation.

You are the best judge of where you are now and whether you might want to change. You may not feel comfortable about deliberately trying to make more of an impression on staff. Again, you might feel you are losing something of intrinsic interest to you if you neglect whole areas of the course in order to concentrate on what you believe is coming up in the exams. As one student said:

> *'It's a pity because there are things I'd like to spend much more time reading around. But it's a luxury I feel I can't afford right now because the only way I see of getting the degree I want is to concentrate on these things that I know I'm.going to have to answer questions on.'*

Perhaps also you might feel somewhat uneasy at being too selective, you might not feel confident if you didn't try to revise everything. And it is not unknown for cue-seekers to come disastrously unstuck in the exam room because the topics they've predicted and concentrated their revision on have failed to come up!

One thing I am quite sure about is this: the more you talk to your fellow-students about your course, and what you are learning, and the problems you encounter, the greater will be your cue-consciousness and your understanding of your situation. And the better you understand your situation – what you might want from it and what it might want from you – the better you are able to decide what to do about it. And what to do about it is whatever suits you best.

If you understand your situation, you may or may not be able to improve it. If you don't, you definitely won't.

Follow-up activities

1 Think back over your answers to the questions in this chapter. Seek out further information where your answers have not been as confident as you would wish.

2 What are your thoughts and feelings about your department as a place in which to study and learn? (Or, if you are a distance learner, about the college/department with which you are studying.) What are its good points and bad points? If you have time, try writing out a one-page review of the department such as you might send to a friend who was considering applying to study in it. (You might use the three main headings I have used in this chapter.)

3 Consider also getting some of your fellow-students to write their own one-page reviews of the department. Hence you might learn even more about your 'situation' by discussing one another's possibly different viewpoints.

4 If you can get students in *other* departments to do likewise, you might learn even more. (It's often difficult to see what's special about one's own situation until one sees how greatly it differs from someone else's.)

5 If you do decide that you and your department are not really suited, by all means consider changing. But make sure you are not jumping out of a frying pan into a fire. Investigate the alternatives with care, e.g.

- Talk to your personal tutor
- Talk to students in the department you think you might prefer
- Ask them some of the questions about the social and learning climates and about the assessment system that you've considered in this chapter
- Ask to see some of their assignments and the kind of comments they get from their tutors
- Skim through some of the key books they are using
- Speak to some of their tutors
- Ask to sit in on some of their lectures/seminars/practicals

Make sure you weigh up the costs of changing (perhaps including the need to repeat a year) against the extra benefit you might hope for from working in the new department.

4

Getting organized for learning

'I was totally carried away at first with the freedom. There was absolutely no pressure on me to do anything at all, so I did very little. Although I didn't want to be over-burdened, I did miss the routine of the grammar school. Looking back, the first year seems a bit of a boozy haze. Quite a few of my friends didn't make it. I managed to catch up, fortunately – but it was a hell of a sweat.'

Are you organized? Few of us feel we are as organized in our work as we should be. We suspect others work more efficiently and don't waste time like we do. And yet we often have a strong suspicion that the different ways we organize ourselves reflect some basic differences in our personalities. Could we really change our ways? And would we feel comfortable doing so, even if we knew how?

What needs organizing?

In this chapter, I want us to consider what might be involved in getting organized for learning. The plain fact is that students who are well organized are generally more successful than those who are not. The underlying issue in this chapter is whether you believe that trying to get more organized might enable *you* to be more successful.

To begin with, here are a number of concerns that students have expressed to me about their study habits. Tick any that you feel would also be true of *you*.

- 'I feel I'm probably not doing as much work as I should.' ☐
- 'One week I find I'm doing nothing at all, and then the next I'm suddenly up to my eyeballs.' ☐

- 'I seem to plod on from one task to the next, with very little idea what tasks lie up ahead.' ☐

- 'I often just feel too tired to think about studying.' ☐

- 'I put things off until a deadline is right on top of me.' ☐

- 'Whatever task I'm working on, I'm forever wondering if I really ought to be studying something else.' ☐

- 'I find difficulty getting started; I keep putting it off.' ☐

- 'I can't seem to concentrate on study for very long.' ☐

- 'I can't find a really satisfactory place to study in.' ☐

- 'I'm way behind, and I wonder if I'll ever catch up.' ☐

- 'How am I supposed to fit studying in with all the other things I've got to do in my life?' ☐

Taking responsibility

For most students, organizing their own learning only becomes a problem when they arrive at college. At school, teachers made many of the decisions they are now being expected to make for themselves. Even students who've worked for several years before coming back to study will often unconsciously expect things to be as they were in school.

Consider the following matters which, at school, were probably all decided for you by teachers. Which are you now expected to take *more* or *total* responsibility for?

	More	Total
● Which topics in the course to put most effort into	☐	☐
● Where to find suitable learning materials	☐	☐
● Which class sessions to attend	☐	☐
● How much time to spend on private study	☐	☐
● When to schedule time for private study	☐	☐
● Which assignments to tackle	☐	☐

	More	Total
● By when to complete assignments	☐	☐
● Deciding how well I am doing on the course	☐	☐
● My physical fitness	☐	☐

If you are like most students, you will find you are taking more, if not total, responsibility for many of the items on the list above. And all of them have a bearing on how successful you will be in college work.

So we now have a list of responsibilities and a list of problems that can arise in the process of trying to meet those responsibilities. If you want to avoid the problems, you'll need to make some sort of a stab at *planning* and *organization*. You will need to plan what needs doing and organize things so that it does get done.

Several aspects of your life as a student and learner need planning and organizing. Many of them are reflected in that list of student laments we looked at earlier on pages 54–55. The main ones, which I want to concentrate on in this chapter, are:

● your lifestyle

● your learning resources

● your time

● your study sessions

These are, in fact, all interconnected. But they are worth considering one at a time.

Lifestyle

Most people's lifestyles have to change when they become students. If you are coming to college, you will be meeting and learning to work with new people – some of them with power over you and many of them with values that may clash with yours. You may be finding your way around a new area, perhaps living in it, perhaps even away from home for the first time. You may be faced with questions of accommodation, money management, and relationships with family and friends that have never much concerned you before. On top of this, you will need to keep properly fed, fit and healthy – because studying makes demands not just on the mind but also on the body.

Even distance learners and mature part-timers will face many of these problems – often struggling to keep a decent balance between the competing demands of study, family responsibilities and their full-time jobs.

There is insufficient space to explore all such lifestyle issues in this book. So I have picked out three that affect most students and that can benefit from a certain amount of planning or organizing:

- improving your working conditions

- keeping healthy

- relaxing

Improving your working conditions

It's worth giving some thought to the kind of surroundings you would like to live and study in. You may not have a choice in this, but there may be improvements you can make.

To begin with, do you live alone or with other people? If you live with other people, are they also students? If not, do they understand the nature of your work and the demands you are facing? If you have any problems at all with the people you are living with, try telling them what effects they are having on your work. Listen to how things seem from their point of view, and try to reach some sort of workable compromise.

And have you found a place where you can study? If you can study undisturbed at home, that may be the ideal place. You'll have all your reference materials to hand and be able to leave your work out between one study session and the next. But maybe home is not a comfortable place to work or maybe you enjoy seeing other people around you studying as well. In that case, you may prefer to study in a library or in some other public room in college.

Some students prefer to stick to one study place. That place then becomes so associated with studying that they find they can slip into the right frame of mind the moment they sit down. Others like to feel there are two or three such places they've got used to studying in.

You need your study place to be well lit, properly ventilated and neither too hot nor too cold. You also need a desk or table, and a chair that is comfortable enough to sit in for longer than you might normally be sitting in a chair. And can you ensure that you aren't unduly disturbed by other people's noise?

Look back over the last four paragraphs about working conditions, and <u>underline</u> any items you may be able to organize better.

It's almost impossible to get perfect conditions, but one can often improve them. And do review them from time to time because things can gradually change for the worse without our noticing.

Keeping healthy

If you want to study well, you need to keep healthy. Yet there are many ways in which becoming a student can put some people's health at risk. In particular I am thinking of the effects of lack of sleep, change of diet and inadequate exercise.

Sleep

Our concentration on study tasks can be much affected by how much sleep we have. It's worth trying to understand how your sleeping affects your learning. If you find difficulty getting to sleep, it may be because you've been overstimulating yourself (whether with tea and coffee, intellectual endeavour or other pursuits) during the evening. Give yourself time to unwind before trying to sleep, e.g. by watching television or practising some relaxation technique such as those mentioned on page 60.

If you really can't get to sleep after lying in bed for an hour or so, don't just lie there fretting about being sleepless. It's usually better to get up and do something, e.g. read a novel and try to sleep again later. An occasional 'poor night' won't hurt you, so long as it doesn't become habitual. If it does, then seek advice from your doctor.

Food and drink

Many young, full-time students appear to live on a daily diet of fried something-or-other and chips (especially chips) washed down by copious quantities of beer. Many others appear to survive on thin air. As one student told me: 'We all drank so much it filled us up and we hardly noticed if we hadn't anything to eat.' So some students put on weight they could well do without and others lose what they can ill afford.

To think and learn effectively, you need a *balanced* diet. This doesn't mean anything fancy – just wholewheat breakfast cereals, bread (preferably wholemeal), potatoes (preferably not fried) and green vegetables, fruit, beans and rice, cheese, fish (again, preferably not fried), chicken and (occasionally) red meat. The important thing is to have a *varied* diet. You can't exist on muesli any more than you can on fish and chips or cream buns.

Such a diet is not necessarily more expensive either. A tin of baked beans with wholemeal toast or a potato baked in its jacket, together with a glass of orange juice, is both cheaper and more nutritious than battered fish and chips and beer. A couple of litres of water a day (not in the form of tea or coffee) are also vital to keeping mind and body working well. There are many books on how to eat cheaply but nutritiously – e.g. Jenny Baker's *The Student's Cookbook* (Faber and Faber, 1996) or Katherine Whitehorn's *Cooking in a Bedsitter* (Penguin, 1991).

Perhaps the key questions here are:

1 Is your weight about the same as that of most other people of your height and sex?

2 Is your weight stable?

3 Are you eating a varied diet?

If your weight is fairly steady at about the right level for your height, and you are eating a varied diet, you probably have no cause to worry. All the same, it might be worth your while picking up a leaflet on healthy eating from your doctor or local health centre. What gets into your stomach will have a lot to do with what gets into (or doesn't get into) your mind.

Physical exercise

Most students coming from school are used to taking some form of physical exercise (however grudgingly). Unfortunately, they often drop it once they start in college. Mature students may have dropped it many years earlier. This is a pity, because regular exercise can have many beneficial effects on your studying. It can improve your digestion, help you sleep better, get rid of tensions (both physical and mental) and even, by improving your circulation and oxygen flow, enable you to think better.

Apart from all those benefits, if you find a form of exercise you enjoy, you can look forward to it as a refreshing change from sitting hunched up over your books or crammed into lecture rooms.

Do you take enough *regular* exercise at present – e.g. jogging, vigorous walking, swimming, dancing, team sports, etc.? (If not, consider how you might organize yourself to do more.)

Any exercise is better than none at all. But you will do your heart and lungs (and the rest of you) most good if your exercise increases your pulse rate and breathing rate and makes you sweat. Twenty minutes of this, two or three times a week, may be all you need. But if you are over-weight, haven't taken exercise for some time or have any reason to be suspicious about your health, get your doctor to check you over first.

Relaxing

Studying can be a stressful occupation if you do it properly. It can be even more stressful if you realize you are *not* doing it properly. You need to be able to recognize when you are feeling stressed, anxious or tense. Is any part of you tense at this moment, for example? Are your shoulder muscles tight? Are your legs crossed uncomfortably? Are you biting your lips or clenching your jaws? If not, do you sometimes tense up like this – when reading, in lectures, when talking to other people? If so, why? And does it interfere with your studying? Do you get backache or eyestrain or headaches?

It is difficult to learn effectively if you can't get reasonably relaxed. There are various ways of doing this. You can stretch, and move around, and get up and walk about more frequently during study sessions. You can flop out and listen to soothing, tranquil music. You can read an entertaining novel that 'takes you out of yourself' for an hour or two. You can get away and have a good time with friends who can get your mind off your problems. Regular physical exercise is also a help.

Yet another approach is to learn some *relaxation techniques*. There are many such techniques and many books about them, for example Laura Mitchell's *Simple Relaxation* (John Murray, 1987). What they mostly have in common is some focus for your attention that pushes all other (potentially agitating) thoughts out of your mind.

I'll mention just one such technique here. We can call it 'focused breathing'. It is quite simple, though you'll need to practise it every day for some weeks before you start getting maximum benefit. All the same, it should be enjoyable and helpful right from the start.

Practising focused breathing

Start with short sessions (say, five minutes twice a day) working up to as much as fifteen minutes per session over the course of three or four weeks. Here's what to do:

1 Choose a certain time (or two times) each day when you will practise the technique. (This helps set up the habit.)

2 Find a place where you will not be disturbed.

3 Make yourself comfortable, sitting up in a chair or lying on a bed or on the floor. Loosen any tight clothing. Tense up all your muscles then let them go limp.

4 Close your eyes and concentrate on your breathing.

5 Make sure you breathe in by making your belly expand before your chest.

6 Breathe deeply and slowly in and out.

7 As you breathe in, hear the word 'IN' in your mind. Elongate it ('I-NNNN') to cover the time your lungs take to fill.

8 As you slowly breathe out, hear the word 'OUT' – or 'OUUUT', again keeping time with your breath.

9 Pause before breathing in again, and so on.

10 *Don't* leap up and start beavering away the moment your relaxation session is over. Ease yourself out of it gradually, as if coming round from a deep sleep, and have a good (but gentle) stretch.

Learning resources

In order to learn, you need access to certain resources. Art students will need access to paints and clay and studios; biology students will need access to chemicals, specimens and laboratories; and so on. But the learning resources all students will need access to are *printed materials* and *other people*. So that is what I want to concentrate on here. How might you organize yourself so as to make the best use of these resources?

Using libraries

Whatever printed materials you need for your course, it is unlikely you'll be able to afford to buy them all. So getting access to them will depend on your ability to use libraries. Unfortunately, many students seem to see the college library as nothing more than a quiet place in which to write an essay, or sleep off the effects of last night's hangover.

Libraries can put a vast wealth of information at your disposal. Most of this will take the form of books, pamphlets, journals, computer databases, etc. But some libraries may have gramophone records, audio and video cassettes, drawings and paintings, slides and photographs, microfilm of old newspapers, multimedia CD-ROMS, access to the Internet (World Wide Web), and so on.

How many libraries?

In any one area, there is usually more than one library. The more libraries you can get access to, the greater your chances of getting the material that will help you learn.

For instance, which of the following might have material that could be useful to you?

- A library in your department ☐
- Other departments' libraries ☐
- Your own college library ☐
- The library of another local college ☐
- A local branch of a public library ☐
- The main branch of your nearest town/city library ☐
- The library of a government department ☐
- The library of a local business or voluntary organization ☐
- The library of a local society (e.g. historical, nautical or photographic, etc.) ☐

Some of the above libraries will be more useful or accessible than others. If your department has a library, the material in it may be relevant but nevertheless too specialized for you. Your own college library may cover some of your needs. But library budgets have been much reduced in recent years and you are unlikely to find copies of the main texts for your course. You may find it useful to join your local public library also. Even if they don't have the book you want on the shelves, they may be able to get it reasonably quickly from another library through the inter-library loan system.

Whether you can get access to other local 'private' libraries mentioned on the list above may depend on your powers of persuasion – and perhaps a letter of introduction from your tutor. Obviously, if you work for a local business or voluntary organization, or belong to a local society, this will give you access to its library. If you are a distance learner, you will probably be sent all the materials you need. If not, you may need your college to help you get access to a suitable library.

Using a library

To get the best use out of a library, you need to know:

- What subjects it covers

- What kinds of materials it contains (e.g. just print, or more?)

- How to find out whether it has (or can get) what you need

- Where to locate the material on the shelves

- What the borrowing arrangements are

- What photocopying, faxing, computing and other facilities it offers

- How to get information on the above topics

There is no point my saying much more about libraries here. They differ so much, as will the needs of the various readers of this book, that too much of what I might say would be irrelevant to your needs.

In fact, as part of your 'induction' to college, you may already have had some kind of guided tour of your own library. You may even have been deluged with information about all the facilities available locally. My own experience, however, suggests that though such introductions are well meant, they often do little but add to the 'information overload' that students suffer in their first weeks in college. You will probably find you need to hear much of it again later – when you have a *purpose* of your own in getting access to library resources.

The best way to find out what your library can do for you, and how to get the best use out of it, is to *ask the librarians*.

Learning from other people

Not all learning is to be found in books and the like. You can also learn from other people. And they don't have to be older than you, or more experienced, or even as knowledgeable as you are about your subject.

Some human learning resources

Consider the following list of people. Which of them might be helpful to you in your learning?

- The tutors of my courses ☐
- Tutors of related courses ☐
- Student-counsellors in college ☐
- Librarians ☐
- Other professional or technical staff around college ☐
- People I work with in my part-time or full-time job ☐
- Local experts/enthusiasts in the community ☐
- People in the community who can give me access to special source materials or practical work ☐
- Family and friends ☐
- Other students on my course ☐
- Students who've been through the course before ☐
- Students on related courses ☐

I am sure you will have ticked quite a few boxes and decided there are plenty of human resources you might draw on – even if you are studying

at a distance. Doing so effectively may take a certain amount of orga-
nizing, though – even if you are studying on campus. For example, your
tutors will be used to running group sessions – lectures, seminars, lab
work, and so on. But you may want them to respond to your individual
needs. This will require that you go out of your way to make an appoint-
ment with the most appropriate tutor (unless you feel it can be dealt with
adequately by button-holing her or him over coffee – or exchanging email
messages).

It will also be helpful to think in advance about how you are going to
explain your problem or difficulty. Such planning may be all the more
important if you are seeking help from tutors or other people with whom
you do not normally have much contact. Organizing yourself to get support from other people is important to any kind of learning. If you are
doing a materials-based course (e.g. by distance learning) it is absolutely
vital (see Chapter 8).

Students as learning resources

I shall leave you to think about how and what you might learn from most
of the people on the list above. And I do say quite a lot about tutors as a
learning resource in the chapters ahead.

I want to turn now to what I believe to be the most valuable learning
resource any student can have (with the possible exception of some
tutors) – and that is *other students*. Throughout this book, you will find I
am urging you to get together with other students – not just, as you
must, to form an audience for a tutor but to learn from one another's
ideas and insights, and to give one another moral support.

**Here are some comments made by students about the kinds of ben-
efits they've gained from working together. Tick (1) any benefits
you'd *like* to get more of yourself and (2) any you think you *might* be
able to get by working more closely with fellow-students on *your*
course.**

	1	2
A *'There's always someone who's understood a point that I've missed and who can explain it to me better than the tutor did. And I often do the same for others.'*	☐	☐

	1	2

B *'I can never get over the fact that even when I've looked at an issue from what seems like every conceivable angle, there's always someone else who's got a plausible alternative approach.'* ☐ ☐

C *'Just finding out I'm not the only one who's having difficulty has been a great consolation to me.'* ☐ ☐

D *'I like comparing approaches to studying – how do the others timetable their work, how do they set about tackling an assignment problem, and so on.'* ☐ ☐

E *'The commitment to meeting regularly has just been a great incentive to getting on with the work.'* ☐ ☐

F *'I think I've got most out of discussing one another's essays and the marks and comments we've got – and using that to suss out what the teachers think is good or not.'* ☐ ☐

G *'It's made me more confident about speaking up if there's something I don't understand in a lecture or demonstration. You don't risk the lecturer thinking you're a solitary thicko, because others in the group will always back you up and say they don't understand it either.'* ☐ ☐

H *'We help each other take a broader view of the course because we've all got our different interests.'* ☐ ☐

I *'Revising together for the exams – that's when it really all paid off.'* ☐ ☐

I hope you have ticked several comments in column 1, suggesting benefits you would welcome (and maybe you've thought of a few other possibilities). How many boxes you've ticked in column 2, indicating which benefits you think you might actually hope to enjoy with fellow students on your course, is another matter.

In some colleges, or in certain departments within a college, the learning climate discourages student collaboration. The students may see themselves as competitors. They kid one another about how much work they're doing and try to keep vital information from one another – even to the extent of hiding essential library books. Alternatively, they may feel no sense of belonging to a group. They just split up and go their separate ways after every group session, without even sitting around for a cup of coffee together.

Distance-learners students, studying at home, may also face problems in getting together with other students – especially if their course has few other students in their immediate locality. Very often they can do so, however, with the help of whoever is running the course. As it happens, several of the comments on the list above come from distance learners, talking of what are usually called *self-help groups*.

Starting a self-help group

Even in the most unpromising circumstances it is usually possible to find three or four fellow students with whom to get together as a self-help group.

Setting up such a group may take a bit of organizing at the start. Who are the members? When/where/how often/and for how long a session will you meet? Or can you 'meet' only by telephone or email? How will the agenda for discussion be decided? And so on. There may be a certain amount of coming and going of members in the early days, until you settle down with a group that can really *work* together rather than just chatting (valuable though that may be in addition). But once the group is established, members are likely to find it so supportive that relatively little conscious effort is needed to keep it going.

You'll notice in Chapter 11 that I talk about a special role for the self-help group when examinations approach – as a 'revision syndicate'.

Organizing your time

Time is a very precious commodity for students – more fleeting than most of them realize. College years are shorter than ordinary ones, usually comprising only about nine or ten months. Take away the vacations and a college year may pass in the twinkling of an eye. Worse still, your college may run short (e.g. 'modular') courses. If so, you won't be able to take your time getting organized. With the end-of-course exam perhaps 10 weeks after you start, you'll need to hit the ground running.

Hence the need to think about organizing your time and planning your studying. If you don't give sufficient thought to what you want to achieve and what others are demanding of you, your time will vanish before you've been able to attend to the study tasks that most need your attention. Realistic planning demands that you think ahead and make decisions about how you intend to spend your study time. Realistic planning also demands that you keep your plans fairly flexible – study tasks often take more time (and, just occasionally, less) than you expect, and priorities change over time.

For which of the following periods of time would *you* feel happy about planning exactly what study tasks you will tackle each day?

- A year at a time ☐
- A term/couple of months at a time ☐
- The coming month ☐
- The coming week ☐
- One day at a time ☐

Most students will feel that a week at a time is about the longest period for which they would try to be very precise. I remember certain students at my own university who produced imposing charts detailing what they would be doing for the next twelve months. They frightened the life out of me at the time. (I was also curiously unnerved by the row of pens those same students invariably wore in the breast pocket of their jackets.) However, I had at least moved beyond the 'one day at a time' mentality of some of my colleagues which, even then, struck me as much the same as not planning at all.

The year ahead

Though you may settle for the *week* as your detailed planning unit, you still need to plan each week against the whole year ahead. So, at the beginning of the year, ask yourself:

- What do I want to achieve by the end of the year?
- What will others be demanding I achieve during the year?
- What weekly classes will I be expected to attend during the year?
- How frequently will I be expected to hand in assignments, etc.?

- How demanding does my 'required reading' load appear to be, compared with other courses I've experienced?

- What milestones or events must I prepare to meet at fixed times during the year, e.g. exams, field trips, the start of a 'sandwich' period away from college, a summer school, completion of a project or dissertation and so on?

- How will these milestones or events affect the amount of time I have to spare for other study activities around that point in the year?

- Are there any other foreseeable events in my life (e.g. a change of job, moving house, having a baby) that might reduce the time I have available for study in certain periods?

- During which parts of the year does my study time look like being under most and least pressure?

You might want to mark up a calendar to show the milestones and fixed events, together with a reminder as to when your time is going to be under greatest and least pressure. And you will almost certainly want to display such information prominently in your pocket diary or electronic organizer.

How confidently could you answer such questions for what is left of your present college year?

Knowing what is likely to happen over the year as a whole should help you plan for shorter periods – the next term, the next month, the next week, tomorrow. Obviously, the nearer the period for which you are planning, the more specific your plans can be.

Planning week by week

Here are some suggestions as to how you might set about planning your study one week at a time:

1 Photocopy a number of timetable sheets, showing seven days of the week each divided into, say, hourly blocks of time from 9 a.m. to 10 p.m., with your regular study commitments (lectures, lab work, meeting of self-help group, etc.) already marked in.

2 Fix on a regular time in the week (say, Sunday evening) when you sit down and plan for the coming week.

3 Check with your long-term diary or calendar to see which milestones or fixed events may demand some of your time in the week, e.g. assignments to be prepared for.

4 Make a list of study tasks that *must* be accomplished during the coming week, e.g. prepare a presentation for Friday's seminar; draft outline of essay; write up lab notes.

5 Make a list of study tasks that *could* be tackled (and should if you can make sufficient time available), e.g. review difficult topics from past weeks.

6 Decide how many hours you can devote to private study next week. Here we are talking about time that is not already earmarked in your timetable as 'committed time'.

If you're like most full-time students, you'll probably have somewhere between fifteen and thirty hours of committed time already filled in on your timetable. Students of arts/social science-type subjects are likely to come off fairly lightly, with perhaps fifteen to twenty hours of lectures and seminars. Science-based students, however, are liable to have another ten to fifteen hours of laboratory work in addition to a similar lecture load.

So, if an arts-based and a science-based student both decide to devote a similar number of hours to private study during the week, the latter will clearly be working a much longer week. However, some research indicates that students tend to have a certain number of hours they intend to devote to study each week, e.g. 40 for a full-time student, 12–15 for a part-timer. The more of these hours get taken up by classes or other teaching, the less they will spend learning on their own.

Private study time
Only you can decide how many hours you need to or wish to spend on private study. Remember, however, that you can't devote all your time to study. You still have other obligations – not least to ensuring you have plenty of social life, exercise and relaxation. Might it be reasonable for you to aim to cover both committed time and private study within an average working week of forty hours? (There may, of course, be weeks when you want to spend more or less time on study.)

Few colleges give any guidance on private study time. Some on-campus tutors think their students should reckon to spend about as much time on private work as they do in tutorials and seminars, some two or three times as much. What do yours expect?

Your plan for the week
Anyway, let's say you have decided how much time to devote to private study in the week ahead. You can complete the sequence 1–6 we started opposite, with four final steps:

7 Decide how much time you will allocate to each of the 'must do' tasks you listed in 4 above; and how much, if any, you can allocate to the 'could do' tasks listed in 5.

8 Take one of your timetable sheets and mark it up to show which of your tasks you will be tackling during which of your sessions of free time.

9 At the end of each day:

- review what you have accomplished during that day

- note anything you wrote on your timetable in 8 that has *not* been completed

- check what you have timetabled yourself to do the following day

- decide whether your timetable needs to be changed in order to finish any uncompleted tasks (or for any other reason)

- make any necessary alterations to your timetable for the days ahead

10 At the end of each week (perhaps just prior to 2 above), reflect on how your actual week has compared with what you timetabled. Don't fret if you haven't kept precisely to your timetable. Just be sure you know *why* you haven't – and decide if you need to do anything about it in planning *next* week's timetable. (Back again to 3 above!)

Which of the following is most like *your* reaction to the approach to weekly planning I've outlined above?

- I don't think it would work ☐

- I haven't got the right kind of personality ☐

- I think it would take up too much time ☐
- I think I might try it ☐
- I do something very much like it already ☐

You might find it helpful to discuss your reaction with other students (and possibly a tutor) – especially if it is a negative one. All I can say here is that I know of many students who started off thinking this method would not suit them who have ended up boasting about how much time it saved them, how much better their results were and how much more self-confident they feel simply as a result of always knowing that they've made plans for the workload that lies ahead.

Planning for vacations

Don't forget to do it. You'll want to take some rest and recreation, perhaps catch up on a number of neglected personal or domestic chores, maybe even take some paid employment. But don't regard vacations as holidays. They are your best opportunity to:

- get more fully to grips with aspects of the course that have caused you problems over the previous weeks
- read more widely around your subject than you normally have time to do
- prepare for the topics and tasks that lie ahead of you

And don't just gather together a pile of books with a vague resolve to 'do a bit of work'. Set yourself some *specific study tasks* and make a weekly timetable as usual. Perhaps you won't be studying for more than a couple of hours a day, unless you are revising for exams. But you'll get more satisfaction from a small amount of time well organized and well spent than from grandiose ambitions that you somehow never get round to implementing.

Organizing your study sessions

With a well-planned study timetable, you should be able to start each day knowing what you are going to do in your private study sessions. But some students will say: 'Even when I know what I've planned to study, I still don't seem to get much done in the time.' Such a student's typical 'study evening' may well go something like this:

Finishes eating (and chatting) about 7.30 p.m. (Had intended to finish at 7.00 p.m.) Sits down at desk but spends first fifteen minutes jumping up and down to fetch papers and books, sharpen pencils, wind clock, etc. Begins to write. Finds pen needs a refill. Goes to borrow ink from friend downstairs. Finds friend with group of students debating relative merits of two tennis stars. Stays to state point of view. Some time later remembers the awaiting study task. Goes back to room. Works solidly for next twenty minutes. Suddenly remembers a recently acquired CD. Why not play it as background music? Attention now shared between CD player and reading. Begins thinking about weekend. Goes out to telephone friend. Returns to discover it is nearly 10 p.m. and still nothing much done. Next forty minutes spent frantically (but hopelessly) trying to make up for lost time. Tells colleagues next day that the evening was spent studying – and remembers only how exhausting and frustrating it all was.

Does this ever happen to you?

To a greater or lesser extent it must surely have happened to all of us. What can we do about it? How might we organize our study sessions so as to make them as productive as possible? I think there are four main things to be considered here . . . preparing, getting started, concentrating and reviewing.

Preparing

You'll have started your preparation for a study session by writing down what task you are going to tackle. And the more *specific* you can be the better – e.g. not just 'Read some statistics' but 'Read and summarize Chapter 5 of *Statistics Without Tears*.' You may have continued this preparation by thinking about what you want out of the session while you were doing the washing-up or walking from your last lecture. Perhaps you'll even have thought of some little treat for yourself when you've managed to accomplish what you set out to do – e.g. watching TV or visiting.

You will also need to ensure you have with you all the texts, writing paper, pens, pencils, etc. that you are likely to need for your study session.

Getting started

The best way of getting started is to get started. Don't hang about waiting for inspiration, or you may be waiting for ever. Don't just sit there – *do* something.

But make sure it is something relevant to the task in hand. Beware of getting distracted into some other task (even if it's another 'must do' task) that isn't so urgent.

You might begin by reviewing your lecture notes on the topic you are dealing with. Or you might write down the main points you remember from the last piece of work you did on that topic. In fact, it is often a good opening gambit to spend the first few minutes of any study session reviewing what you last did on the topic. And preferably write something down.

If you still can't get started, ask yourself *why*. I usually find it's because something else is playing on my mind – something that I have not yet admitted to myself is more important or worrying than what I had planned to do right now. I then can't settle to the task until I've done something about what is worrying me.

Find out what's blocking you and, if possible, fix it. Maybe all you need is a brisk walk or a hot drink. Maybe your room is too hot and stuffy. Maybe your relaxation technique (see pages 60–61) will get you going. You will sometimes conclude that you must abort a session. But don't let yourself off the hook easily; and be very sure about why you are doing it and how and when you are going to make up for it.

Concentrating

Once started on your study session, how do you keep yourself at it? To begin with, you need to know how you work best.

For instance, do you prefer to work:

- for short, intense periods with frequent breaks? □
- for long periods without a break? □
- differently according to topic and type of task? □

People have different concentration spans, and you may find that yours varies considerably according to what sort of work you're doing. So don't be surprised if you sometimes find yourself so totally immersed in what you're doing that you've lost all track of time, while at others you are having to get up and stretch your legs every half hour or so.

Looking for interest

Obviously, the best aid to concentration is *interest* in what you are doing. When you are busy with intrinsically interesting deep-level learning (see Chapter 2), you won't even think about having to concentrate. The problem arises mostly when you are engaged on some task that seems irrelevant or too difficult, or that creates anxiety – e.g. about which aspects of it you'll be tested on tomorrow. You'll then drift into unsatisfying surface-level learning and you'll be easily distracted. And, very often, the more you try to *force* yourself to concentrate the more difficult you'll find it – because you'll be thinking about concentration rather than about the meaning of what you are studying.

If you find yourself losing concentration, make yourself think about the meaning of what you've been working on. Review the work so far. Ask yourself questions about it. Raise questions that you want to answer before the end of the study session. Think about how it fits in with other work you've been doing or will be doing. Remind yourself why you need to complete the task.

The need for variety

All the same, you can't concentrate for ever, even on something that deeply interests you. You'll need to get up now and again, walk around, stretch, make a cup of coffee, focus your eyes on something more distant than the page or computer screen in front of your nose. But don't spend so long at it that you lose the thread of your thoughts.

And many students find they can concentrate for a longer period overall if they tackle several different tasks rather than one – say, two or three quite different tasks in an evening rather than sticking with one throughout. How about you? Maybe a change will be as good as a rest?

Building up your concentration

Some students find that even with a subject they are interested in, concentration is an ability they have to build up gradually. If you can't concentrate for an hour at a time, set yourself a goal you can accomplish in half an hour. If even that is too difficult, set yourself fifteen minutes' worth of work. Once you've proved to yourself that you *can* keep hard at it, even for a short spell, you should be able to lengthen your concentration span. But again, don't sit too long over it – as easily happens with work on a computer – so that your eyes and neck and back get severely strained. By all means carry on thinking, but do get up and stretch every 30 minutes or as often as suits you.

Reviewing

Don't finish a study session without reviewing it. Did you accomplish what you planned? If not, why not? And what do you plan to do about it? Whether you achieved what you planned or not, where do you go from here? Is that the end of the piece of work? Or shall you need to do more? And, if so, what and when?

Incidentally, if you do have to leave a topic unfinished, it's often a good idea to leave off at a point of interest – so that returning to it will seem a happier prospect than if you'd left it just when the going got tough.

Your review, which need only occupy five minutes out of an hour's session, is often the *vital* element that determines how much value you get out of the session.

When you've finished, stop and relax for a while before your next study session. Or, if you are not going to do any more, go off and reward yourself for your efforts.

It takes time and trouble to get yourself organized for learning. But, in the long run, muddling along takes even more – and the results won't be as satisfying.

Follow-up activities

1 Discuss some of the issues raised in the Lifestyle section with fellow-students. How do your views compare?

2 If you are on campus find out about the local facilities for medical care and for student counselling. Find out whether there are any useful leaflets – e.g. on health, diet, relaxation techniques.

3 If you have any troubles that might interfere with your studying, *tell someone* – a personal tutor, counsellor or whoever seems most easy to talk to. Such people are there to help.

4 Use your library to track down some of the books mentioned in the References at the end of this book. If they don't have one you want, find out how they can obtain it for you.

5 If you are worried about how you are using your time, keep a diary for a week or two. Make a careful record of how much time you spend on each activity each day. Consider what changes you might want/need/be able to make if you are not satisfied with the amount of time you devote to studying.

6 Consider getting together with fellow-students and forming a self-help group. (You could begin by discussing some of the issues raised in this book – especially the section in this chapter about working with other students.)

5
Developing a strategy for reading

'There's no end to it. I'll never get through this lot. So many books on exactly the same topic, and they don't even tell you which are the best ones. I bet they haven't read half of this stuff themselves.'

Those are the reactions of a first-year student on being presented with the reading list for his course. You may have felt similarly yourself – especially if you realize that the list is 'just for starters' and more items keep getting added as you go along. Not for nothing is degree-level study often called 'reading for a degree'. Even if you are learning with computers (see Chapter 8) you are likely to find they give you plenty of reading to do.

Managing your reading

If you are to keep on top of your reading, you will need a strategy – a way of coping with the seemingly endless flood of material. You'll need to think about:

- the kinds of material you have to deal with
- how you can be more selective in dealing with it
- what your purposes might be in reading it
- the best ways of setting about that task

What must you read?

The kinds of material you need to read will depend upon your subject. Which of the following will be part of your study reading?

- Basic textbooks that are essential reading because they teach all the key topics in the course ☐

- Supplementary textbooks for optional use if you wish for an alternative viewpoint on certain of the topics ☐

- Primary source materials – e.g. government reports, novels in a literature course or court reports in law ☐

- Research reports ☐

- Academic journals intended primarily for specialists in your field but perhaps containing articles of value to students working at your level ☐

- Lighter journals – e.g. *New Scientist* or *History Today* ☐

- Collections of 'readings' – articles and other materials drawn from a variety of sources ☐

- Instruction manuals – e.g. on how to operate equipment or follow procedures ☐

- Professional or trade journals ☐

- Newspapers ☐

- CD-ROMs ☐

- Computer-assisted learning ☐

- Multimedia ☐

- Email or computer conferencing messages ☐

- World Wide Web resources ☐

You will, no doubt, have ticked at least one or two of the items on the list above. And you may have added some of your own. (If you are following a materials-based course, you may have added other sorts of materials.) You should also know which ones are compulsory reading and which are optional.

The realistic student soon accepts that it is impossible to read everything that might be relevant in his or her subject. (Even tutors won't claim to have done that!) One eventually recognizes that, beyond a certain point, reading more on the same topic is no substitute for standing back from the topic and coming up with one's own perspective on it.

Remember: the goal of learning at your level is *not* to repeat back everything that everyone else has said on your subject but to *create* and express a coherent picture of your own.

How to cope with the quantity?

Students of the arts and social sciences usually find themselves with more to read than students of, say, mathematics, science and engineering. But most students feel there is too much to read in the time available. You may have a shrewd suspicion that half of it may be not worth reading – it won't add much to the picture you already have. But how can you tell which half without reading it all? So how are you to sort the chaff from the grain and keep on top of your reading?

Some students try to give their closest attention to every book and article (or World Wide Web site) that ever gets suggested to them. But they find new material being suggested faster than they can cope with the old.

Selectivity

There is no virtue in reading fast just for the sake of it. Efficient reading means being *selective* about what you read, and then reading it at whatever speed is appropriate to the nature of the material and to your *purpose* in reading it.

If your purpose is understanding, speed reading is *not* appropriate, as Woody Allen once reminded us: 'Yes,' he said, 'I've just done a speed reading course. Read *War and Peace* last night – all 900 pages. About Russia, isn't it?'

The quickest way to deal with your reading is not to learn speed-reading techniques – though most of us can benefit sometimes from making ourselves read faster than usual. Rather it is to cut down on the *amount* you need to read.

To begin with, here are some possible ways of being more selective about the material you need to read. Tick those you think you might be able to apply.

- Ask your tutors for a list of 'recommended reading', if you haven't already got one ☐

- Ask your tutors to indicate which parts of the recommended materials are most relevant (and why) if they haven't already done so ☐

- Keep alert for hints and cues about relevant reading that are dropped by tutors in lectures, and assignment feedback, etc. ☐

- Ask fellow-students which of the materials they have found most and least useful (and why) ☐

- Ask students who have been through the course ahead of you ☐

- Share out the reading with two or three fellow-students and regularly report to one another on what is worthwhile ☐

- Note which books/materials are most regularly mentioned in other books as being important ☐

- Skim very fast through recommended books (e.g. five to ten minutes per book) with a view to deciding which (or which parts) might repay closer study and which can be ignored. (More about this one later.) ☐

- Whatever you are reading, keep asking yourself 'Why am I reading this? What am I getting out of it?'; and be prepared to drop it if you can't give yourself satisfactory answers ☐

However selective you are, you'll still *find yourself with plenty to read.*

Being selective is an essential aspect of efficient reading. The other two are knowing your *purpose* in reading and being able to read in an *appropriate manner.*

Purposes in reading

We can have many purposes in reading – from amusing ourselves or just killing time at one extreme, to seeking deep understanding of an author's thinking and experience at the other.

Consider some study reading you have done within the last week. Which of the following different purposes might you have had in mind? Tick as many as apply.

- Browsing through material to see whether any of it might be worth reading more carefully □
- Looking for specific factual information □
- Looking for help with a particular essay or assignment topic □
- Finding instructions on how to do something □
- Getting a quick overall picture of a subject □
- Memorizing as many of the details as possible □
- Looking for the author's underlying assumptions or bias □
- Trying to follow a complex argument □
- Identifying the author's main ideas □
- Comparing the author's viewpoint with other viewpoints or with your own experience □

I hope you found that exercise straightforward. I've known students who have found it difficult to see any purpose beyond the fact that their tutor told them to read pages so-and-so to so-and-so before their next session.

From purpose to approach

Whichever different purposes you've identified they should have led to different approaches to the reading. Clearly, for example, if you were simply 'browsing through material to see whether any of it might be worth reading more carefully', you would not (by definition) read it as carefully as material in which you were trying to follow a complex argument.

But what sort of approach is suited to what kind of purpose? Many students seem to know only one approach. They start with the first word of the text and they plod on regardless until they reach the final word. Then they stop. They apply this approach whatever their purpose – or perhaps because they haven't thought about what their real purpose might be. Such an approach is rarely suitable for any study purpose.

I am now going to describe a reading strategy which you should be able to *adapt* to suit different purposes and different kinds of material. It is often known as SQ3R.

SQ3R – a flexible strategy

SQ3R stands for the initial letters of *five* aspects of studying any printed material – whether a whole book, a chapter within a book, an article, or whatever. These are:

- Survey
- Question
- Read
- Recall
- Review

SQ3R is a flexible strategy. You can apply it in different ways to different materials, to suit your own purposes. The basic stages, however, are these:

1 Try to get the general drift of the material you are looking at by carrying out a quick preview or *survey*.

2 While you are doing your survey, start asking yourself *questions* that you might expect to find answers to if you think the text worth reading more carefully.

3 *Read* the text carefully (if it seems worthwhile).

4 When you have finished reading, try to *recall* the main points.

5 Check how well you've recalled by going back to *review* the text.

Let's look at these one by one:

Survey

If you get good at surveying, you'll be able to *deal with* far more books and articles than you'll ever need to read in detail. I only wish that one could deal with computer-based materials in the same way. But often (e.g. with multimedia or CAL packages) it is impossible to get a general overview before committing oneself to screen-by-screen scrutiny.

Surveying a book

A book, for example, is likely to have several features that are well worth a quick preview, e.g.:

- cover ☐
- title page ☐
- list of contents ☐
- preface/foreword/introduction ☐
- final summary/conclusions ☐
- index ☐
- bibliography/references to further reading ☐
- final glossary ☐
- the body of the text itself ☐

Tick any of the above features you *actually* looked at before you started reading the text you are working on *now*.

This book does not have a 'final summary/conclusions' or a 'final glossary' but it does contain all the other features. I believe you will be getting more out of your detailed reading if you at least glanced at them first.

The cover
You know the old saying: 'Never judge a book by its cover.' Fair enough, but you can still learn much of value from it. It can tell you:

- The general subject area – the title of the book.

- The particular 'slant' or 'angle' – the sub-title, if any, or any descriptive 'blurb', usually on the back cover.

- The author's name and his or her background and qualifications or 'track record' that might help you decide whether he or she is likely to be someone whose views are worth your attention.

How much of this information can you get from the cover (back and front) of the book you are looking at *now*? If you haven't done so already, please take a look before you read on.

Since you are now reading this, I assume you've looked at the front and back cover of this book – and nothing you saw there has put you off giving the book some more of your attention! Obviously you noticed that the book is about studying *and you may have felt that its approach might be a fresh one. You will also have noticed the name of the author – which you may or may not know from some of his other books mentioned on the back cover – and what his qualifications are supposed to be for writing the present book.*

Sometimes, the information you get from the cover will be all you need to decide that a certain book is not suited to your needs. So you will be able to cross it off your list and go straight on to surveying other candidates for your precious reading time.

The title page
The title page is the next thing to survey. It may tell you something about the author that is not mentioned on the cover, e.g. qualifications. And, on the reverse, it may give information that may or may not be useful to you about:

- when the book was first published
- whether it is an import/translation or a 'home-grown' product
- how long it has been in print
- how frequently it has been reprinted
- when it was last revised or updated
- how recent is the edition you are reading
- how up-to-date it is likely to be
- the name and address of the publishers

The front of my title page gives you little information that you will not already have gleaned from the cover. The reverse of the title page, however, gives you a full publishing history of the book – enabling you to decide whether it is likely to be up-to-date enough to suit your needs. It also gives you the publisher's name and address.

The list of contents

This is another set of pages that you should never ignore when making your preliminary survey. The contents list tells you what topics the author is dealing with. In addition, it sometimes gives you some idea of how she or he has organized them – main topics, sub-topics and so on.

Look back at the contents list for this book:

1   How many topics does the book offer?

2   Are there any topics you would have hoped to see covered in a book on studying but which do not seem to be given a chapter of their own?

3   Is there any indication of the sub-topics dealt with in each chapter?

4   Do any of the missing topics you picked out in (2) seem to be among the sub-topics indicated in (3)?

Your survey of the contents list should have told you there are eleven main topics and indicated the sub-topics dealt with in each chapter. If you'd been looking especially for certain topics that seemed to be given neither chapters of their own nor sections within other chapters, e.g. 'How to memorize' or 'How to finance your studies', you may have decided the book was not one you wanted to spend more time on.

So your survey of the contents list should give you some idea of what is dealt with in the book. And it may give some clue as to how the topics are related to one another. Later, if you read one or more of the chapters, you may need to return and survey the contents list again.

Perhaps your purpose in picking up the book was simply to look for references that might help you answer a specific question? If so, your preliminary survey may well end at this point. You'll have seen whether or not the book is likely to contain anything of relevance to you. On the other hand, as sometimes happens, you may have found the contents list unhelpful. It may have left you unsure whether or not the book would suit your purpose. In either case, you may now want to survey . . .

The index

An index, of course, is a detailed list of the topics covered, usually printed at the back of the book. I say 'of course', but I have met many university students who act as though they are unaware that indexes exist. Either that, or they have simply never felt the need to consult one. Hand them a book and ask whether it has anything to say about, for example, brainstorming, and they'll willingly spend the next ten minutes flipping through the pages in search of the magic word – when a five-second glance at the index would have told them that the book has nothing to say on the subject!

Not all books have indexes. But most educational books do, and the index can save you a lot of time. It reveals at once whether a subject is dealt with and, if so, tells you the numbers of the pages on which you will find it mentioned. Some indexes are better than others, i.e. more detailed. But almost any sort of index is better than none.

Does *this* book say anything about brainstorming?

As you'll have seen from my index, 'brainstorming' is mentioned on pages 170–2, 205, 217, 230.

Again if you're looking for something very specific, your survey may end with the index. You may go straight from there to the few bits of the book that seem of relevance. Otherwise, if your interests are wider and your survey of the index shows that many of them are dealt with, you may need to survey . . .

The preface/foreword/introduction

Most books have a page or two at the front in which the author introduces the book. Again, students often completely overlook it. This is a pity because these introductory remarks can often tell you, e.g.

- the main themes of the book
- how the book is structured
- how it relates to other books in the same area
- in what ways it is different
- whether you're going to like the author's style
- who the book is written for

- how the author imagines readers might want to use the book

- what you might be expected to get out of the book

In short, the preface may help you decide whether the book is worth reading, and even *how* you might best set about it.

What kinds of information do you get from the preface of *this* book?

My preface tells you why I think the book is needed and something about what you can expect from it. It states the underlying theme (reflective self-development) and the key questions that readers will need to consider. It also describes my intended readers and defines some important terms. Finally, it makes a few suggestions about how to use the book.

The glossary

Many books have a glossary (often near the end of the book, but sometimes at the end of relevant chapters) – a list of key concepts, together with their definitions. The only glossary in this book, at the end of Chapter 10, concerns the key verbs used in essay titles.

In surveying a glossary, you may want to ask yourself, for example, how familiar you are with the concepts mentioned and whether you want to use the index to find the pages on which some of them are discussed.

The bibliography/references

The kinds of book you are studying will usually mention other books and articles or computer sources. They may be mentioned page by page throughout the book, or in a list at the end of each chapter, and almost certainly at the end of the book. The author may mention material he or she has consulted or quoted from. He or she may also recommend you to further reading, at the same level or at more specialist levels.

A preliminary glance at the titles mentioned may help you decide how useful the book you're surveying is likely to be.

In this book, my references to other materials are mostly at the end. Check to see what form they take. Do they seem sufficiently helpful? Would they raise any expectations about how suited to your purposes *this* book is likely to be?

You'll notice that none of the items I mention is actually aimed at students. But I say why they may be of interest to you. And I tell you where some of them are referred to elsewhere in this book. My remarks may have confirmed that this book is likely to be on your wavelength, or may have cast doubts on it.

One more vitally important item to survey:

The body of the text itself

As part of your survey, it is worth leafing through the pages of the book from front to back. While leafing through you might:

- Notice the headings and sub-headings
- Read the end-of-chapter summaries (if any)
- Notice how the text is laid out on the page
- Look at any charts, pictures, tables, etc.
- Read the occasional sentence

Obviously, very little of what you see will stick in your mind at this stage. That is not the point. What you are doing is getting a *feel* for the book – its style and its structure. And does it seem right for you? Is it, or sections of it, worth reading more carefully?

If you haven't done so already, leaf through the whole of *this* book. Follow the suggestions above. What would such a survey tell you that might influence you in reading (or not reading) this book?

I can't tell how leafing through this book may have influenced you. But, for example, some students may have been encouraged on seeing that it is structured around frequent activities – while others may have been put off by this feature! Again, you may have decided that some chapters look more relevant to your needs than others.

So, I have mentioned nine aspects of a book you might want to survey. The books in your particular subject may not always have all of these features. On the other hand, they may have special features of their own (e.g. appendixes) that may be worth surveying.

The point of surveying or previewing a book is to decide: *What's in it for me?* In the process, you'll have raised many other questions also.

About how many minutes do you think it might be worth devoting to surveying the kind of book you normally have to deal with?

How long you spend on surveying or previewing a book will depend on how big it is and how likely it is that you are going to have to read it whether you want to or not. My own guess is that you'd need at least five or ten minutes to do a worthwhile survey of quite a small book – but probably not more than thirty minutes even if the book is to be the backbone of your course.

Very well, let's say you've invested an adequate amount of time in surveying the whole book. You expect to reap the benefit when you come to reading it. Do you start to read sentence by sentence from the beginning of Chapter 1 (or of whatever chapter you've decided is most worth your attention)?

You may do. But it may not be the best way in. Perhaps you might consider spending just a couple more minutes at the survey stage. . . .

Surveying a chapter

Before you begin each new chapter, consider surveying it again. But *rather more carefully* than you did when getting an idea of the book as a whole. Pay special attention to:

First and last paragraphs
Authors often use them to give a survey of what is to come, or a summary of the chapter's main conclusions.

Summaries
These may appear at intervals during the chapter, as well as (or instead of) at the end.

Headings
Many authors take considerable care in using their headings and sub-headings. They use them to show how their ideas hang together – the structure of their argument. Sad to say, many students more or less ignore the headings. They try to read a highly structured teaching text as though it were a novel.

Obviously, headings should tell you what *topic* is dealt with in each section or sub-section. But there's more to them than that. For instance:

What can you tell from the relative size, boldness or typeface of headings? (Look, for example, at the headings over the next few pages.)

The headings are graded so as to tell you how the topics are related to one another – which are sub-topics within some wider topic. Thus, above, the three headings in light italics indicate three aspects of the topic suggested by the heading above them.

Look out for the grades of heading in surveying a chapter or an article. Since they tell you which topics belong under which, they are the key to the author's structure of ideas. They are a clue as to what is in the author's mind.

Most texts will have two or three grades of heading. They will decrease in size and/or boldness – from chapter heading to section heading to sub-section heading and so on. If the author has got his or her ideas sorted out, each heading of a certain grade will refer to all the material that follows until you come to another heading of the same grade. That is, anything with a lower-grade heading is always an aspect of the previous higher-grade heading.

Check back through this chapter again from the beginning, looking at the headings. How many grades have I used? Do they follow the rule I've suggested in the last two sentences of the paragraph above?

Including the main title of this chapter, I have used five grades of heading. Each heading follows the rule. Here are some of them again, arranged to show how the topics are related:

Grade 1 # Developing a strategy for reading

Grade 2 ## SQ3R – a flexible strategy

Grade 3 ### *Survey*

Grade 4 **Surveying a book**

Grade 5 *The cover; The title page; The list of contents; etc.*

You might like to finish this survey, by checking through the remaining headings in this chapter.

As you may judge from the amount of space I have devoted to it, I think that *surveying* a book, or a chapter or an article, is a vitally important aspect of dealing with texts. What do you think?

Anyway, I hope you'll agree with me about the next aspect of the SQ3R strategy of 'Survey–Question–Read–Recall–Review':

Question

Whenever you begin the careful reading of a text, try to be sure you have in mind a set of questions you want answered. Questions are a great stimulus to learning. They give your reading more *purpose* and they help you read more critically and with greater alertness. You become an active searcher after meaning rather than a passive soaker-up of words.

Your own questions

In fact, questions should already have started coming into your mind the moment you began your initial survey. Not just the big one – 'What's in this for me?' – but also a variety of others.

In surveying the book as a whole, your questions are likely to be rather general ones. Glancing at the title page, preface and list of contents, for instance, you might ask yourself:

● What do I know about this subject already?

● Is this book sufficiently up to date?

● Will it be as helpful to *me* as its preface suggests?

● Why does the author think it worth giving a whole chapter to such-and-such a topic?

Even questions as general as these can be of some help in deciding how to or even whether to tackle the book. But when you turn from surveying the book as a whole to surveying the chapter you are about to read, your questions will become more *specific*.

Headings are always likely to bring questions into your mind – if only 'What does it mean?'

Look at the next three headings (pages 94–95). What questions do they bring to your mind?

'Other people's questions' might lead one to ask:

- Which other people?
- What sort of questions?
- What use are they?

'Questions in materials-based learning' might suggest:

- What's materials-based learning?
- What's special about the questions?
- What's this got to do with my sort of learning?

'Read' might suggest:

- Don't I know how to do this already?
- Is the author going to discuss new ways?
- Why is the section so short?

Here is a list of some aspects of a text that might raise useful questions in one's mind when one surveys it before beginning to read:

- Headings
- First and last paragraphs
- Summaries
- Calculations
- Tables
- Diagrams, maps, graphs, etc.
- Technical terms
- Author's style

Other people's questions

You are not the only source of useful questions. Sometimes your tutor may suggest questions to bear in mind while reading a particular chapter or article. Or your colleagues may pose questions – or make comments that are easily rephrased as questions – about chapters they have had to struggle with. For instance, a fellow-student might say: 'The article is supposed to be spelling out five ways of explaining criminal behaviour, but I'm damned if I can see more than three that are really different.' And you ask yourself: 'I wonder if I can?'

Sometimes, the most useful outside source of questions is the book or article itself. The author will often pose three or four questions at the beginning of a chapter – as a means of indicating where he or she is taking you. And you will be looking for answers to emerge as you read on. Likewise, it is quite common for authors to begin a paragraph with a question – which they then go on to explore.

Unfortunately, students often fail to notice that the author has posed a question. So their reading is not so inquisitive as it might usefully be.

Questions in materials-based learning

Many students nowadays are working on materials-based learning courses, e.g. distance, open, flexible, resource-based, or computer assisted learning (see Chapter 8). Such students often depend on self-teaching packages – sometimes just printed texts, sometimes a combination of print, audio- and video-tapes, computer-based materials, or whatever.

If you have worked through any such packages, you will know that they tend to have one thing in common with the book you are reading now – lots of questions!

The frequent questions – often called activities or exercises – play an important part in materials-based learning (as in this book). If the author has thought them out well, they will help ensure that you work through the materials with understanding. So the author will ask you to apply the ideas she or he is presenting – by recognizing examples, offering examples of your own, solving problems, relating the ideas to your own situation and so on. As in this book, the author's comments usually follow in order to give you feedback.

What would you guess is the chief *purpose* of such questions and feedback in materials-based learning (and in this book)?

The chief purpose of the questions and feedback is to help you learn and understand. But, if you think about it, this way of learning can teach you more than just the particular subject matter it involves. It can also help you develop this habit of reading questioningly.

Whatever you are reading – textbook, article, computer screen or whatever – it can be worth asking yourself: 'What are the *most crucial ideas* in this material and what questions would I insert into it if I wanted to get readers to make use of them?' And, if you are reading questioningly, as one question is answered, others will arise.

Normally, the answers to your questions will emerge as you work through the text. What action might you take if you could not find satisfactory answers to an important question within the text?

If it was an important question (like 'Where can I get hold of some of this materials-based learning material in my subject?'), you might feel inclined to make a note of it and seek the answer elsewhere – from a tutor, a colleague, librarian, another book or whatever.

So, one of the most important reasons for making a preliminary survey is that it gives you a chance to start asking questions. These will add purpose to your reading. At first you may find question-raising difficult or a bit artificial. But, if you practise for a while, you will soon do it automatically. Read questioningly, and the questions will come.

After *survey* and *question*, we can consider the third aspect of the strategy of SQ3R (Survey–Question–Read–Recall–Review). If your initial work suggests that the text is sufficiently suited to your needs, you will want to read it more closely. (And, if it is lengthy World Wide Web resource or other computer text, you may want to print it out to ease your task.)

Read

What we are talking about here is what students often call *careful* reading. I am suggesting that this should be the *third* step, not (as many students seem to think) the first and only step. It should have been preceded by a lighter, faster kind of reading – while you were surveying and starting to raise questions.

There's quite a bit to be said about reading carefully and I've devoted the next chapter to it. So I won't say much more here. I'll only remind you that careful reading means reading actively and critically. Your job is not to be a kind of vacuum cleaner sucking up other people's words. Rather you should be looking for the main ideas behind the printed words and *testing* each one against the author's other ideas, against other experts' ideas and against your own experience and sense of logic.

Certainly, in all your reading, you should always be asking yourself questions like:

- Does this text have what I need?
- What does this statement really mean?
- Are these facts or opinions?
- How does the author know those facts (or justify his or her opinions)?
- What alternative facts or opinions might be worth considering?
- How does it all relate to my experience?

Don't make notes at the 'read' stage. Don't even underline or highlight passages, even if the book belongs to you. Note-making is part of the fourth aspect of SQ3R.

Recall

The business of studying a text should not end with the reading. Unless you are gifted with an unusual memory, you will forget fifty per cent of even the most important ideas you have read within minutes of putting down a book – unless you make an active attempt to *recall* them. In general, the surest way to remember ideas is to *use* them – and trying to recall them is the first way you can do this.

The value of recall

Make regular attempts to recall during your reading. This will aid your learning in three main ways:

- You'll *concentrate* better because you'll know you have the task awaiting you

- You'll have the chance to *remedy* any oversights or misinterpretations

- You'll be kept *active* because you must come to grips with what you have read and summarize it in your own terms

Could you get these benefits simply by going back and *reading through the text again*?

Well, it's your opinion, but I rather doubt if rereading can be a full substitute for recall. As you surely know, the fact that you can recognize ideas once you see them again is no proof that you can remember them without the text in front of you – let alone express them in your own words.

How often to recall?

Once you have embarked on your reading, then, you may find it helpful to:

- pause from time to time
- close the text
- tell yourself the main ideas you have met so far

How often should you pause?

Think of the kinds of text you have to read. How frequently do you feel you should pause and try to recall the main ideas?

There is, of course, no one right answer to this question. It all depends on the kinds of text you need to work on, what demands they make on you and what your purpose is in reading them. However, here are a few general remarks:

It is probably not helpful to stop and recall at the end of every sentence, unless the sentences are long and complex (as I know they sometimes are as in, say, philosophy texts). One normally needs to read at least a paragraph in order to see what the author is getting at.

With a long or complex paragraph it can sometimes be worth looking away from the text for a few moments to see if you can summarize the main point in your own words. But don't make a routine of stopping after *every* paragraph (or even couple of paragraphs). To do so might hinder you in keeping up with the momentum of the author's argument.

Recalling after each section is probably OK for most purposes. Might it be sensible, for example, to pause and take stock each time a new main heading comes up? Thus, you might be reading several pages before you stop and try to recall the important ideas you've met in the chapter so far.

You will, of course, be wanting to pause at the end of a chapter, section or article and recall *all* the important ideas you've met since you started reading. But if your chapters or sections are long or rather complex, your recall may be frustratingly hazy unless you have paused once or twice somewhere along the way.

So there are no golden rules about how often to stop and recall. It's something you'll have to decide. And what you decide will no doubt differ from one text to another and how you are feeling at the time.

Make notes

Don't just *think* your recall. *Write down* the key points. Make brief notes of the main ideas and any details that seem important to you. Even the sketchiest note-making is better than simply letting half-formed recollections drift through your mind. It is easy to be over-confident about how clearly one has understood a section of text – until one tries to pin it down in words (or as a diagram). Besides, you may need a *record* of what you have read. We look further into note-making in Chapter 9.

How much time on recall?

You may need to spend quite a sizeable proportion of your SQ3R time on recall. How much will depend on the kind of material you are reading. If the material is difficult to understand, or if you feel you must memorize it, you may spend more time recalling and reviewing than reading.

Anyway, don't be surprised if you find yourself spending *at least half* your SQ3R time on recalling with certain texts. If the ideas in the text are important to you, the time will not be wasted. In fact, the time-wasting students are those whose aim is simply to get another reading chore out of the way. Even if they understand while they read, they will lose that understanding unless they follow through – by recalling and reviewing.

Review

Here your purpose is to get feedback as to how well you have recalled. Never try to convince yourself that you have recalled everything of significance, and recalled it correctly. Always view again to make sure. (With some computer-based material, this will not be very easy.)

How to review

You may think it better to work on the assumption that you've probably missed something – rather than on the assumption that you've probably got it all right. One way of reviewing is to do a quick repeat of the previous four aspects of SQ3R. That is:

1 *Survey* the general structure of the section or chapter. (Look again at the headings and any summaries.)

2 Remind yourself of the *questions* you asked. (Can you answer them all? Do any new questions arise?)

3 *Reread* the text to see that you've recalled everything of importance.

4 Complete your *recall* by filling any holes and correcting any faults in your notes.

If you are working on a book or other printed material that belongs to you, you may also want to underline or highlight some of the important passages.

Now let's apply some of this to the chapter so far:

First recall the main ideas (i.e. think of the headings) – making some brief notes from memory. *Close the book* while you do this.

Then review to check how well you've recalled. Follow the four steps above, or whatever approach suits you.

How satisfied were you with your recall? More than you usually would be, I hope. But probably not as well as if you'd tried to recall after each of the sections (assuming you didn't).

The five aspects of SQ3R have been used by thousands of college students who have reported favourably on how helpful they have found the strategy. Almost certainly you could benefit too.

But one point must be stressed. SQ3R is *not* a formula or recipe to be followed blindly. You must be prepared to bend it and adapt it to suit your purposes. At different times you will use some aspects of it but not others. Or you will vary the amount of time you spend on each step. The basic strategy is flexible enough for you to use in a variety of ways and still get useful results.

SQ3R in lectures, etc.?

So far, we've talked about SQ3R only in relation to *texts* – books, articles, computer printouts, etc. What about other types of studying?

In particular, how possible might it be for you to apply *any* or *all* of the five aspects in a *lecture*? Tick the relevant boxes.

	Definitely Possible	Perhaps Possible	Definitely Impossible
Survey	☐	☐	☐
Question	☐	☐	☐
Read	☐	☐	☐
Recall	☐	☐	☐
Review	☐	☐	☐

Compare your ideas with mine:

Survey
Difficult to apply unless your lecturers are willing to tell you where they are heading. Some are, however, and you may think it is worth asking them.

Question
Preliminary questioning may be difficult without the cooperation of the lecturer. But you should be able to think of some general questions as soon as you know of the subject – and you should certainly be able to listen questioningly once the lecturer has begun to speak.

Read

Impossible, of course, unless your lecturers provide you with a copy of their notes or a detailed handout. But you may feel that *listen* serves the same purpose as *read*.

Recall

Definitely possible – and even more essential than it is with texts, since you can't go back and hear the lecture again (unless it's been recorded).

Review

Usually impossible in the strict sense (unless there's a recording). But you *can* check what you recall against what other students thought they heard. And if there are still points you aren't sure about, you can perhaps ask the lecturer.

So, to a large extent, SQ3R is applicable to lectures as well as to texts. I leave it to you to decide in what way you might apply it to other forms of studying – e.g. seminars, practical work, projects, computer-assisted learning or whatever. The basic principle is that, with any potential learning experience, you should get a good enough idea of it in advance to decide whether and, if so, how you might approach it, and to reflect on what you have got out of it afterwards.

> **If you plunge into a learning task without first considering your purpose, you may be wasting your time. And if you don't reflect on it afterwards, you almost certainly will.**

Follow-up activities

1 If your reading lists simply mention texts without any comment on them, ask your tutors to discuss with the class why each text has been chosen – e.g. Are certain texts essential? Do some deal with an aspect of the subject better than others? And so on.

2 Discuss with fellow-students how they are coping with the volume of reading they have to do. How do they select what they will read?

3 Discuss with them whether there are ways in which some of you (e.g. in your self-help group) might save one another's time in reading.

4 Select an article, chapter or other text that you believe you may need to read carefully, and apply the SQ3R strategy. Note how you apply each of the five aspects and how you adapt each one to suit your purposes.

5 Try the SQ3R strategy on a book you must become familiar with. In what ways (if any) do you think it might help you tackle books more effectively than you have in the past?

6
The art of reading actively

'I'd have read it differently if I'd known you weren't
really going to be testing me on it afterwards. 'Cos in
that case, I'd have more, you know, thought about
what it said, and what was the point of it all . . . how
he built up the whole idea. Instead of which I was
just all the time trying to think, "Now, I must
remember that" and "I'm sure they'll be asking me
about this."'

Student on how she tackled a reading exercise

Ideally, you should have read Chapter 5 before starting on this one. If you did, you will have some idea of what I mean by reading actively. It means reading with a sense of *purpose* – critically and with questions in mind. The object of the exercise is not to transfer the words into your mind. Rather it is to interrogate the author, make sense of his or her ideas and decide what relevance (if any) they have for you.

If you did read Chapter 5 earlier, you will surely by now have done a quick survey of this chapter and asked yourself questions about it. If you haven't, do so now. These are the first steps towards reading actively.

I hope that, as a result of your survey, you have some questions that you expect this chapter to help you answer – if only 'Am I already reading as effectively as I need to?'

In any careful reading of a text – whether book, chapter, article, report or whatever – you will probably be trying to do three things:

- Find the *main ideas*

- Pick out the *important details*

- *Evaluate* what you are reading

We'll look at them one by one below. But remember that, in practice, you are likely to be doing all three *at the same time*.

Looking for the main ideas

The most important question you can ask yourself about a text will be *'What's the main idea here?'*

Main ideas can be found at *each level* of a text. Take a book, for example. It will have, perhaps, one very general main idea. You may be able to find that idea by reading no further than the blurb on the back cover.

The main idea of each chapter within a book will be rather less general. Each section within a chapter (or article, report, etc.) will have one or more main ideas – but more specific ones. The main idea of each paragraph will be most specific of all.

If you are to make sense of a text, you will need to pick out the main ideas at each level. Let's illustrate this with some examples.

Below are four *main ideas* from this book.

A 'Effective reading is active reading.'

B 'Main ideas vary from general to specific according to the amount of text they relate to.'

C 'A prime aim in reading is to identify the main ideas.'

D 'Students can develop more effective approaches to studying.'

Which of the main ideas above belongs to:

	A	B	C	D
1 the book as a whole?	☐	☐	☐	☐
2 this chapter of the book?	☐	☐	☐	☐
3 this section (headed 'Looking for the main ideas')?	☐	☐	☐	☐

4 the third paragraph above; starting 'The main
idea . . .?   ☐ ☐ ☐ ☐

---

*The main ideas belong as follows: 1(D), 2(A), 3(C), 4(B). You may dis-
agree with the way I have worded those main ideas. After all, it is
important that you should be reckoning to express an author's ideas
in your own words. However, even if we disagree about the wording, I
expect you were able to identify the level of the main ideas I picked
out.*

The author's plan

If you read a text critically, you may be able to detect how the author has
structured it. What is her or his *plan* – the underlying framework of ideas
around which the text is organized? Maddeningly, you may get faced
with a few books that ramble all over the place and have no coherent plan.
But, thankfully, these are few and it's best to assume that your text probably does have some kind of plan or framework – if only you can ferret it
out.

In particular, you might look for a *hierarchy* of main ideas. That is, can
you see how:

● the main idea of the book (level 1) breaks down into a number of
more specific main ideas . . .

● each of which is the main theme of a chapter (level 2), and each
chapter's main idea breaks down to provide . . .

● main ideas for each of its sections (level 3), and each section's main
idea breaks down to provide . . .

● even more specific main ideas, one per paragraph (level 4)?

In practice, there may be more than one main idea at each of these
levels. That's one of the factors that can make sorting them out more
complicated than it sounds.

The diagram (Figure 1) could illustrate the hierarchy of main ideas
(each disc a main idea) within a small book or a lengthy article or
report:

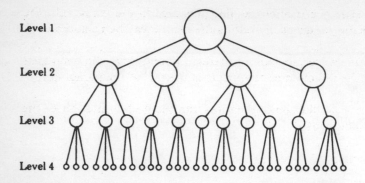

Figure 1: Hierarchy of ideas

The more general main ideas

You will already have got some clue about the more general main ideas (levels 1–3, perhaps) from your preliminary survey of a text.

That is, there are several features of a text that might give you some hint of these, even before you begin to read it carefully. Jot down two or three of them before you read on.

You may have listed: the title, blurb on the cover, author's preface or introduction, summaries, headings and so on. (Headings, in particular, can be a useful guide to the author's hierarchy of ideas – if he or she has used them logically.) All of these can alert you to the more general main ideas.

More specific main ideas

When you come to the *read* stage of the SQ3R approach (see Chapter 5), you are looking for more specific main ideas. You will be asking what the author is trying to get across in each section, even in each paragraph.

Topic sentences

It's quite a useful rule of thumb to assume that your author has put just *one* main idea in each paragraph. Often the essence of this main idea is stated in *one* sentence. This is sometimes known as the *topic sentence.*

The topic sentence is often the first sentence in the paragraph. The author begins the paragraph by stating the main idea, then elaborates on it.

Sometimes, however, the author prefers to build up to the main idea. In such cases the topic sentence appears at the end of the paragraph.

Which sentence would you say carries the main idea in each of the three paragraphs above?

(a) 'It's . . . sentence.'

(b) 'The . . . it.'

(c) 'Sometimes . . . paragraph.'

I would say the sentences carrying the main ideas are: (a) first; (b) first; (c) last.

Do you agree?

Whose main ideas?

There is some scope for disagreement in deciding what the main ideas are. For instance, as the author I know that the main idea I wanted to express in paragraph (a) was in the first sentence. If you were already familiar with that idea, however, the main idea for *you* may have been the one I mentioned in passing in the final sentence. There is always this possibility in reading that an idea that strikes one very forcibly may not actually be the main idea that the author is wanting to get across at that point.

By all means take note of the ideas that particularly appeal to you. But you may need to grasp the text as a whole – perhaps just to see how the idea that interests you ties in with the author's more general themes, perhaps to satisfy some requirements of your tutor. Be careful not to lose the author's drift.

Looser paragraphs

So, the topic sentence may appear at the beginning or end of a paragraph. Only rarely will you find it somewhere in the middle. But what you will come across, from time to time, is the paragraph in which *no* single sentence can be said to carry the main idea. Particularly in fiction or in descriptive writing, the essential idea may be spread out across the whole paragraph. Indeed it may never be stated explicitly at all.

Deep- vs surface-level reading

Researchers have said that students sometimes fail to see the main idea of a text *because they are not looking for it*. They are too busy trying to memorize the surface details to look beyond it for whatever meaning the author is trying to convey. The student I quote at the beginning of the chapter probably falls into this category. Here, another tells how it happens:

> *'In reading the article, I was trying hard to remember it – too hard – so that I could hardly concentrate for thinking how will I be able to remember all these facts, and that must be why I don't remember it. Daft, really.'*

Unfortunately, the less meaning something has for us, the less likely we are to remember it. So, the pressure to memorize something can often be counter-productive – because it makes us unable to relax enough to see the meaning, which is what will make it memorable!

Picking out the details

As well as tracking down the main ideas, you'll need to have your eyes open for the important details. Some students complain they can find the main ideas, but can't tell what might be significant details. Others are so impressed by the details that they fail to see the main ideas. Yet others just don't recognize that there's a difference.

What is an important detail?

On the other hand, students who do see through to the main idea sometimes can't decide what detail is important enough to take note of. What is an important detail? It is one that clarifies, or supports, or illustrates or develops the main idea. It may be an example, a proof, an explanation, an application or an implication. It may take the form of words, or figures, or calculations or of graphs, photographs, maps and so on. Usually there is at least one important detail attached to each main idea.

Sometimes it is a matter of *opinion* as to whether a particular detail is important or not. Ask yourself:

- Is this the best example (or proof, etc.) of the main idea?

- Can I think of a better (and perhaps more memorable) one?

- Do I really need to recall this detail in order to understand and recall the main idea?

If you decide the detail is not very important, you may decide there is no need to take note of it. Or you may think of a better way of your own in which to clarify or support the main idea. Usually an example from your own experience will be more memorable than one provided by the author.

As an example, look at the first paragraph in this section, starting 'On the other hand . . .'

1 What would you say is the main idea?

2 What would you pick out as important details?

3 Can you think of an example from your own recent reading?

---

1 *The main idea of the paragraph is in the third sentence – which remarks that an 'important detail' is one that adds something special to a 'main idea'.*

2 *Probably the most important detail is the set of examples of things that might add this special something to the main idea – that is, proofs, examples, applications, etc.*

3 *If you were able to think of your own example, then this, for you, might count as an important detail.*

Use all the author's clues

One way of spotting important details – and of confirming main ideas – is to keep alert for all the clues the author is offering you. A text does not consist just of words. How the text is laid out on the page may also be important. So too may be the styles of type. Illustrations of one sort or another may offer important information. And Chapter 5 discusses the vital role that headings can play in helping you see how authors are structuring their argument.

Look out for signposts

Headings are like signposts, helping you see your way through the words towards an author's meaning. But there are more signposts the author may have used – both *visual* and *verbal*:

Visual signposts
All of the following are visual signposts – clues that can help you make sense of a text:

● Words printed in *italics*

● Words <u>underlined</u>

● Words in CAPITALS

● Words printed **bold**

● Items listed in a column with numbers or 'bullets' alongside

● Boxed items of text

● Text printed with more space around it than usual

● Text in colour

● Lines of special type across the page

● Numbered paragraphs

● Any others you can think of in the texts or computer materials you normally use

Which of the above have I used in this book, so far as you've noticed?

I have used several of these kinds of visual signpost but not underlining, words in capitals, spaced-out text.

Verbal signposts
You would be wise to keep equally alert for clues that authors give you in their words and phrases. Look out for statements like these:

● 'Firstly . . .'

● 'On the other hand . . .'

- 'Furthermore . . .'
- 'Another example . . .'
- 'Therefore . . .'
- 'For instance . . .'
- 'In much the same way . . .'
- 'What all this adds up to is . . .'
- 'Now we come to an aspect that may seem surprising . . .'
- 'Let us turn aside for a moment to examine . . .'
- 'At this point the argument becomes rather involved . . .'
- 'But this no longer holds true when we look at . . .'

I could go on. And no doubt you can think up many examples yourself. The point is, such phrases are the author's way of telling you that he or she is about to list some details, tell you the implication, qualify an idea, give you an example and so on. They act as *links* between one bit of the author's argument and another. They should help you pick out the main ideas and important details.

Can you see a 'verbal signpost' of this kind in the first sentence after the heading above, beginning 'You would be wise . . .'?

The verbal signpost I was thinking of is the word 'equally'. This word links its paragraph with the previous one by comparing the importance of the two kinds of signpost.

Diagrams, tables, etc.

Many students miss a lot of main ideas and important details because they ignore the author's charts and graphs, tables, diagrams and so on. Some students seem to assume the diagrams are just there for decoration. Others perhaps assume they will be too difficult to understand.

The truth is, an author's illustrations should be read as carefully as the text. Few authors will have used them just to jolly up the text. Textbook authors will normally only use diagrams, charts, and so on, in order to say something that could not be said so easily in words.

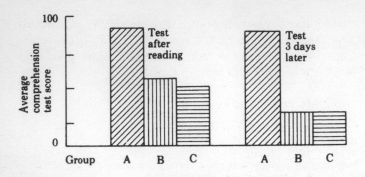

Figure 2

Figure 2 shows the average test scores of three groups of students after a reading experiment in which Groups A and B were given a test with illustrations while Group C was given the same text with the illustrations removed. Only Group A was told to pay special attention to the illustrations.

So which of the following would you say is the *best* reason for paying attention to the illustrations you come across in a book or article?

(a) They may help you to a better understanding of the main ideas and important details you have read in the text ☐

(b) They may make it unnecessary for you to read the text ☐

(c) They may contain main ideas and important details that are not spelled out in the text ☐

(a) is a good reason – illustrations may certainly clarify something in the text. (b) is most unlikely; authors rarely have enough space to be able to make all their points both in words and in pictures, even if they want to. Some points will be made only in words, others only in pictures; so you need to attend to both. (c) is therefore the best reason. An illustration may have been used to save a thousand words.

Dealing with difficulties

I mentioned that students sometimes avoid charts and tables because they expect them to be too demanding or difficult. That may sometimes be the case, of course, but it's no reason for not having a go at them.

This raises a more general point, however. What might you do about any reading difficulties you do encounter – whether with words or pictures? There are several reasons why material might give you problems. Which of these have you come across?

(a) It seems too simple, and therefore boring ☐

(b) The subject matter doesn't interest me ☐

(c) I don't like the author's style ☐

(d) I disagree with the author's beliefs or attitudes ☐

(e) It's full of technical terms I don't understand ☐

(f) The argument is extremely complex ☐

If material really is too simple (a), then perhaps you needn't bother to read it. But be absolutely sure first that you could outline all its essential main ideas and important details. It may just be, especially if the material has been recommended to you by a tutor who knows your needs, that the author is so skilful that the material just looks *simple.*

If the subject matter doesn't interest you (b) and yet the material is required reading, then you have a problem. I only hope that the approaches discussed in this chapter and the previous one will help you to *put* interest into the reading – if necessary by making it a challenge.

If you don't like the author's style (c), try to see past it. Try to recast what he or she is getting at in your own words. If possible, discuss the material with other students who aren't so worried by the style. Similarly, if the author's beliefs or attitudes offend you (d), talk them over with students who are not so offended, and don't let the differences between you and the author prevent you from seeing what he or she is trying to say – even if you fervently disagree with it.

If the jargon is troubling you (e), and the material does not have a glossary to help you out, perhaps you need to start with more basic material. Perhaps you also ought to be using a dictionary of the key terms in the subject. Again, consulting tutors or other students may help, and once you understand the ideas, then the jargon – the technical terms for those ideas – will eventually trip off your tongue without your giving it a thought!

As for the complexity of material (f), one just has to recognize that some ideas and lines of argument *are* difficult to get one's head around. So, read it again (and again), and discuss it with other people.

Sometimes it is possible to skate over a difficulty for the moment, and go on to more straightforward parts of the text. To do so makes some students uneasy, however. And there is always the danger that your lack of understanding of some early part of the material will make it even more difficult for you to understand something that comes later. You may find it preferable to work extra hard on the difficult material, where possible consulting other resources and getting help from tutors and/or other students.

Now, to reinforce a point I made earlier, I just can't resist posing you this exercise. *Without looking back*, see if you can answer these two questions about the illustration I showed you a couple of pages back (Figure 2):

1 What did the illustration actually show?

2 What conclusion might we be expected to draw from the illustration?

Here are my answers:

1 The illustration showed that students who were told to look at the illustrations while reading a text scored considerably higher on a comprehension test than students who were not told to look at the illustrations or who read the text with the illustrations removed.

2 We might be expected to draw the conclusion that students in general will learn more if they pay attention to the illustrations in texts.

I wonder if you had any trouble with that spot-check? If you did, you can always blame me for not actually mentioning the illustration in my text – which is something authors normally do, even if they don't elaborate on it.

This brings us into the third important aspect of reading I want to mention in this chapter: *evaluating* the text.

Evaluating the text

What we are talking about in this chapter is the quality of your understanding. This depends to a large extent on how well you can sort out the main ideas and important detail in what you are reading. But it also depends on your ability to evaluate what you read.

By this I mean you should be a sceptical reader. Don't take anything you read (not even in this book) on trust. To be sure, authors usually know far more than you do about their subject. But that does not mean they know everything you know. Besides, where facts are concerned, few authors get them all right. Where interpretation and opinion are concerned, you can be even more sure that different authors would present different slants. (And those different slants might be equally well worth considering.)

So, examine your authors' statements critically. Look for limitations, exceptions, contradictions, oversights, arguments against those they advance. As one student put it in describing her reading:

> *'You keep stopping to say, "Hang on, that can't be right," or wondering whether this really follows from what they've just said, and why they haven't said anything at all about such-and-such – really, is it all convincing and logical?'*

Let's apply this kind of scepticism to the illustration we discussed a few moments ago. I don't suppose you disagree very much with what I said the illustration *showed*. But what do you think about the *conclusion* I said we might be expected to draw – that is, that students in general might be expected to learn more if they look at the illustrations in their texts?

You may or may not think this is probably true. But can you see any reasons why it might not follow from the evidence presented in the illustration?

There could be several reasons why students in general might not benefit in the same way as the students in the experiment. We might want to ask: Did the comprehension test give undue emphasis to the material contained in the illustrations? Were the ideas in the illustrations also outlined in the text? What sort of material was it? What kind of students were involved? Did the test really find out whether or not students had grasped the meaning of the text or just whether they had noticed easily testable details? Have other such experiments yielded similar results?

There are many more such questions you might want to ask before jumping happily to the conclusion that what happened in one situation (and we're not sure *exactly* what did happen) could be expected to happen as a general rule. In effect, we're back to reading *questioningly*. Ask questions that probe and test what the author is saying. Be especially careful to do this when you *agree* with what the author is saying.

Here are a few examples of questions one might want to ask. Which of them might seem worth asking in the kind of reading *you* have to do?

- What do I know about the authors? ☐
- What facts are the authors presenting? ☐
- Are the facts complete enough? ☐
- Are they sufficiently up to date? ☐
- Are they plausible, e.g. supported by evidence? ☐
- Do the authors distinguish between facts and opinion? ☐
- Do they make clear any bias they may have? ☐
- What exactly are their conclusions? ☐
- Do their conclusions follow from what they've said? ☐
- Would other conclusions follow equally well? ☐
- Do their conclusions make sense of all the evidence? ☐
- How do their conclusions compare with mine/my tutor's/ other writers'/other students', etc.? ☐
- Is the material worth making notes on? (If so, why?) ☐
- Is it worth discussing with someone? (Whom? Why?) ☐
- Have I learned anything that might be of use to me? ☐

- What are the weaknesses I would pick out in the authors' work? ☐
- What are the strengths I would pick out in the authors' work? ☐

I leave you to decide which questions are most worth asking in which contexts. I will simply add that you may find many of them worth asking of lectures *and* computer resources *as well as of texts on paper.*

The essence of evaluating a text (or a lecture) is that you should test what its author says against your own knowledge, experience and sense of what's logical. And even if you feel it all hangs together quite satisfactorily, don't forget to ask the overall, evaluative question that relates it to your own needs: *What's in it for me?*

Where possible, compare your evaluations with those of other students.

Concentration and speed

What I've been saying in this chapter has been largely to do with how to improve one's *understanding* while reading. I've said nothing about concentration or about increasing one's reading speed. In fact, the effort of understanding – trying to pin down an author's meaning (rather than trying to memorize his or her words) – is probably the best spur to concentration. Even so, there are several other factors to take into account, and these are discussed in Chapter 4 (pages 74–76).

There is one kind of text that I often have trouble concentrating on – i.e. text that comes to me on a computer screen. If it runs to more than a screenful, I usually print it out and read a paper version. How about you?

As for speed, I repeat what I said near the beginning of Chapter 5. The best way to cut down on the time you need to deal with a given number of words is to be *more selective* about which of them you need to read carefully. The most important aspect of speed in reading is to be able to change gear – sometimes reading (or skimming, scanning and skipping) as fast as you can (e.g. in surveying or looking for isolated bits of information) and sometimes slowing right down, lingering over an author's turns of phrase or pondering (perhaps for several minutes) the implications for you of a single sentence.

> **Reading is not a race against time. It is better to fully understand one chapter than to half-understand two.**

Follow-up activities

1 Try to ensure you have the best physical conditions possible in which to read, e.g. comfortable chair and table, good lighting, freedom from undue distractions.

2 If you are constantly being held up in your reading by not knowing the meaning of ordinary, non-technical words, keep a good dictionary with you, look up the meaning of such words and make a note of them to enlarge your working vocabulary.

3 Take a book or article that is of relevance to your course and apply some of the suggestions offered in this chapter, e.g. those about evaluating a text (use the checklist on pages 116–117). How useful did you find these suggestions? Can you adapt some of them to your own reading purposes in future?

4 Remember the *recall* and *review* phases that should follow reading (Chapter 5). Apply this to any whole text (book or article) you are reading, as well as to individual sections on the way through. What strikes you as most important about the work as a whole? Which bits are most worth reading again?

5 Whatever you've learned from a text, remember to make use of it (e.g. in discussion or assignments) as soon as possible and as often as possible. This will help make it part of you.

6 Whenever possible, try to discuss things you've read and found worthwhile (or puzzling or annoying) with other people – preferably with fellow-students (and tutors) but, when they are not available, with family, friends or whoever you might be able to interest in the topic.

7

Learning from lectures and other listening

'We have some lecturers who talk at us non-stop, scribbling stuff on the board all the time, and we're still trying to get it down minutes after they've left the room! You're too busy to learn anything. What I like are the small group sessions – not that we have enough of them – where the teacher takes more of a back seat – still guiding, sort of, but you do get a chance to put your point of view and hear what other people think.'

This chapter is about learning by listening. Students spend quite a lot of their time listening to people talk – chiefly in lectures, but also in discussion groups of various kinds, as well as in practical sessions and sometimes in fieldwork. How well you learn in such situations depends to a large extent on how effectively you can listen. So, before we look at the situations themselves, let's consider what's involved in listening.

Are you listening?

Most of us assume that we are pretty good listeners. But how often, when we think we are listening, are we merely 'hearing'? If we are really listening, we are being *active* – we are doing something with what we are hearing. We are thinking about it. Our minds are working on it (not just our ears).

One of the troubles is that we can often think faster than the other person can talk. So it is easy to get distracted by thoughts of our own. In a conversation or discussion group, for instance, we can get distracted by thoughts about what *we* intend to say next.

Furthermore, much of what students have to listen to may be difficult to follow or unappealing. Your lecturers may sometimes speak too

fast or dwell on material you find irrelevant. Other students may sometimes irritate you with the long-windedness of their contributions to
discussion sessions. No wonder there's sometimes a temptation to 'tune
out'.

However, the realistic student is one who knows how to listen – and
listen *actively* – whenever she or he is likely to benefit. This means concentrating on what is being said, and on the way it is being said. The active
listener is looking for *meaning* in what she or he is hearing.

Our listening weaknesses

**Most of us have our weaknesses as listeners, though few of us give
much thought to them. Which of the following weaknesses do you
recognize in yourself – whether in lectures or in discussions with tutors
and other students?**

Selective listening
- Are there some individuals you avoid having to listen to? ☐

- Do you 'tune out' on certain topics? ☐

- Do you refuse to listen to things that might make you feel
  uncomfortable? ☐

- Do you listen chiefly for facts and overlook expressions of
  feeling, opinion or prejudice? ☐

- Do you listen only to what the other person is saying without
  wondering about whether they are really conveying what they
  mean? ☐

Attention
- Do you let your mind wander or pursue thoughts of your
  own? ☐

- Do you spend most of the time thinking what *you* are going
  to say next? ☐

*If you recognize any of these as personal weaknesses, you may want to
take one at a time and try to overcome it. In focusing on one, you may
find that others improve too.*

Learning in lectures

The lecture is still the most common way of teaching in college. In its basic form, the lecturer speaks to you and the other students for anything up to an hour. But none of you speak back. The communication is *one-way*.

Possible benefits

Here are some of the benefits that lectures are sometimes said to be able to provide for students. Which of these 'benefits' would you *welcome* getting from lectures (box A)? Which of them do you *actually* get from your lectures (box B)?

	A	B
● Ensuring that all the basics of the subject are explained to all students on the course.	☐	☐
● Providing an overview of the subject to help students explore the detailed issues on their own.	☐	☐
● Conveying experience (e.g. from research) that is not to be found in books.	☐	☐
● Summarizing books and other materials that students might have difficulty in obtaining or using.	☐	☐
● Adapting a subject to the needs or interests of the students (in a way that no existing textbook can).	☐	☐
● Infecting students with the lecturer's enthusiasm for the subject.	☐	☐
● Demonstrating how an expert in the subject handles it (and thus providing a 'model' for students).	☐	☐

If there are benefits you would like to be getting but are not, perhaps this is something you might want to discuss with other students – and maybe take up with your lecturers. Similarly, if you feel you are not getting any benefits at all. (One of the themes of this chapter, as of several others, is that you may need to take action if you want your situation to change for the better.)

The real world of lecturing

The truth is, many lectures are less beneficial than they might be. There are many reasons for this. Some lecturers are more concerned with covering what is probably an overcrowded syllabus than with ensuring that students are understanding. Some (and in universities, many) have had little or no training in lecturing – and may be nervous, stilted, muddled, tedious or even inaudible. Yet others may be press-ganged into teaching subjects they are not expert in, or into teaching their own subject to students in other departments – without facing up to the fact that the interest of those students in the subject (if any) is very different from that of the students they normally teach. Some, as one student put it, 'seem to regard lecturing as one big chore.'

However, we may hope that standards will improve in colleges now that the quality of teaching is being officially assessed every few years. And, fortunately, not all lecturers are inept or uninterested. Some are able to project their own enthusiasm for the subject, to show sensitivity to what newcomers find difficult in it, and to keep students so involved that, as one student said:

> 'You can tell by her tone of voice that she knows what she's talking about. You can hear her mind at work. But at the same time she's got a light touch – occasional asides and flashes of humour. It's difficult to say how she holds our attention all that time – I mean I'm not all that keen on the subject – but I think her style somehow gives you a lift, regardless of what you might be learning.'

Whatever your lecturers are like, they are part of your 'situation' (see Chapter 3). For the most part, you will have to make the most of what you get. Even the best of lectures require some effort on your part if you are to get anything from them. And even the poorest may yield some benefits if you:

1 Prepare for the lecture in advance.

2 Listen actively during the lecture.

3 Think about it afterwards.

If you've already read Chapter 5, you'll no doubt be able to think of this in terms of the SQ3R strategy discussed in that chapter.

Preparing for a lecture

You'll probably learn more from a lecture if you prepare for it before-hand. Here are some questions that might guide you in this. Tick any that you might apply to the lectures you attend.

- What is to be the topic of this lecture? ☐
- How does this topic relate to others in the course? ☐
- What do I already know about the topic? ☐
- What have I learned in previous lectures that might help me with this topic? ☐
- Have I done any reading or practical work that has been recommended in connection with this topic? ☐
- What *questions* or *concerns* have I about the topic? ☐
- What kind of benefit would I *want* to get from attending the lecture? ☐
- From what I know of the lecturer, what kind of benefit can I *expect* to get? ☐
- Do I want to make arrangements with a colleague to compare notes afterwards? ☐

Obviously, you won't be able to answer any of the above questions unless you can answer the first.

Listening actively

Make a point of arriving in good time for the lecture. If you were to arrive late you might not only disturb your fellow-students and the lecturer but might also spoil your own chances of getting benefit from the lecture. For one thing you might be too late to get a copy of any handout. For another, you might miss the lecturer's introduction in which he or she perhaps relates the lecture to previous ones, explains how it will be structured, or mentions the main themes that will emerge.

Questioning

The key to active listening, as with active reading (see Chapter 6), is *questioning*. As the lecturer talks, you should be constantly asking yourself questions. In particular:

● What is she or he saying?

● What does it mean?

● How does it connect with what she or he has said so far?

● Where is it leading?

● What is the overall structure? (Look out especially for 'verbal signposts' like those mentioned on page 103.)

● What are the main ideas?

● What are the important supporting details?

● Am I getting answers to the questions I had about the topic?

● How might the lecturer want me to use this information?

● What ways might I see of using it?

Evaluating

At the same time as you are asking yourself questions to check that you understand what your lecturer is trying to get across, you should be evaluating what you hear.

Look back at the questions on pages 116–117 to do with evaluating *texts*. Which of them might you be able to use in evaluating lectures also?

With a little rewording, I would say that all of them could be used in evaluating what a lecturer is saying.

One of the questions in that list, you'll have noticed, reads: 'Is the material worth making notes on?' Chapter 9 is devoted to making and using notes, but we'd better say just a few words about lecture notes here.

Making notes

In fact, 'a few words' is about the best advice anyone can give you on writing notes in lectures. Writing notes *can* help you concentrate. But if you try to write too many; then, as one student said: 'You're always one paragraph behind and you're never quite listening to what's being said.'

Aim to record the bare essentials rather than every syllable that falls from your lecturer's lips. Listen for phrases like 'The main difference is . . .' or 'The three chief factors are . . .' or 'The best source on this is . . .'.

Even if your lecturer covers the board with material and seems to expect you to copy it, think twice about how much of it you really need. And keep your ears open while you are writing, because the lecturer may be commenting on the material as he or she writes and the comments are sometimes more significant – and more worth noting – than the material itself.

Concentrating

Many lectures go on far too long. Active listening and questioning should help extend your concentration span, even with a dull lecturer. But we all have our limits.

How long can *you* listen to your lecturers before you feel your concentration beginning to lapse?

Obviously it will depend on the lecture, the lecturer and your mood at the time. But few of us can listen even to an above-average lecture for more than twenty or thirty minutes without our attention beginning to lapse.

There is no easy answer to this. Perhaps you can shift around a bit in your seat, or even get up and stretch. A more radical approach might be to interrupt the one-way flow and ask the lecturer a question.

Thinking about it afterwards

As soon as possible after the lecture – and definitely the same day – try to *recall* it. Can you remember the general issues or themes that were dealt with? What were the main ideas the lecturer put across? What supporting detail did she or he give you? Did it all hang together? Did you find it useful and satisfying? Unless you do something to bring the lecture back to mind, you will probably forget most of it within a few days.

From recall to review?

Such an attempt to recall is also a helpful check on how useful your notes are. If possible, recall the lecture in company with a fellow-student, perhaps with members of your self-help group if you have one. See how their notes differ from yours. Can you see ways in which you might make notes that will be more useful to you in future?

With a lecture, it is impossible to have the 'review' step used in the SQ3R approach to reading (see Chapter 5) – or not unless someone has taped it. But if two or three students get together they can usually combine their recollections to recreate a pretty complete impression of the original.

Another way to ensure you get best value out of a lecture, and improve your chances of remembering it, is to *apply* its ideas as soon as possible. Maybe the lecturer suggested some problems to think about or some follow-up practical work? Maybe you're expected to read up on the topic as a preparation for the next lecture? Maybe you have to complete an assignment in which the lecture material is relevant? If you haven't actually been given such follow-up work, look for your own ways of using the lecture's ideas – whether in this subject or in another one. Practice with ideas is what enables you to make them your own.

Towards better lectures

If you and your colleagues have real difficulty in agreeing what the lecturer was talking about, you may decide to go and see him or her about it. If you explain your difficulty tactfully, your lecturer may not only be able to sort it out but also see ways of putting things across more clearly in future. Many lecturers simply have no idea how little their students are understanding. As one student said:

> 'They'll sometimes say at the end, "Now, is there anything you haven't followed?" but I mean, you can't say, "Well, none of it really!" now can you?'

Do you have any lecturers you'd like to see adopt new approaches? Can you see any ways you and your colleagues might help them change?

Some lecturers you may decide are beyond reprieve. Perhaps they make it clear they have no interest in doing the job well. Others you may feel are uneasy about their performance and would like to improve – if only they can do so without losing face. You and one or two colleagues might be able to help them – not, of course, by criticizing their weaknesses but, more positively, by emphasizing the kinds of difficulty you encounter and describing (if appropriate) the approaches used by other lecturers that you have found helpful in overcoming such difficulties. Perhaps this a subject worth discussing with your colleagues?

Lectures *vs* audio-tapes

With materials-based learning (see Chapter 8) lectures are often replaced by audio-tapes. But rather than simply recording their lectures, many teachers take a different, more conversational approach on tape – perhaps along the line of a radio talk or discussion with experts, or maybe weaving together a set of interviews. Although you can't ask the speaker questions at the end of the tape, you can at least get him or her to repeat any difficult bits as often as you like!

Learning in small groups

To do them justice, many lecturers have already realized that traditional one-hour, one-way lectures may not fit in with their aims of helping students learn to *think*. So – where class size permits - they have devised a variety of alternative forms of teaching, especially ones that get students talking back to the tutor and to one another. At the very least, they leave plenty of time for questions at the end of their lectures – or even keep their lecture plan so flexible that they can restructure it in response to student questions *on the way through*. Yet again, they may break up the lecture with small-group discussion (see the student quote on page 42, top). And of course they may do more and more of their teaching in small group sessions that are clearly not lectures at all.

The variety of small groups

Small group learning may take many forms. For example, which of the following kinds do you have in your course(s)?

- Discussion in pairs or small groups *within* a lecture ☐

- A brief (ten- to fifteen-minute) lecture followed by extended discussion ☐

- An open discussion of some topic the group members have prepared for in advance, e.g. by reading ☐

- A discussion based on a presentation by a student ☐

- A group whose task is to solve a problem or carry out some experiment or practical activity ☐

- Groups structured in such a way that members can share their views and experience with two or three other people before discussion by the group as a whole ☐

- Role-plays or simulation games ☐

- Groups which set out to explore people's values and feelings as well as (or rather than) intellectual issues ☐

Some of the types of group I've mentioned above will overlap with one another. But there are no doubt many more kinds of small group than I have mentioned. You may, for example, do group work by means of 'computer conferencing' (see Chapter 8) but that would involve you in reading rather than listening.

The benefits of small-group learning

Such small-group learning can offer many benefits – apart from giving you a break from solitary private study and the remorseless grind of listening to lecturers lecturing. Small-group work can help you, for example, to:

- try out your ideas on other people
- hear other people's ideas
- share your feelings about a subject and/or about learning
- get practice in 'doing' the subject (e.g. philosophy or law) as opposed to reading, writing and hearing about it
- realize that you are not the only one having difficulties
- develop a closer relationship with the tutor

- practise the important skills of communication (especially listening and giving and receiving feedback)

More about listening skills

Small-group sessions go by various names in different colleges – seminars, tutorials and workshops are three of the commonest. One thing they all have in common is that they make far more demands on your listening skills than do lectures. For a start, there is far more chance that other people will notice whether or not you are listening. Even more importantly, you will be talking back. So your listening has to be good enough for you to give other people appropriate feedback and to make relevant remarks yourself.

Small-group learning highlights one of the main tests of active listening – whether you can tell someone what they have just said, to their satisfaction, but *in your own words*. It also gives you practice in working out what people *mean* by what they are saying (which may be something rather different).

More listening weaknesses

So here is another list of potential listening weaknesses that can prevent you getting the best out of group learning. These are concerned with *interruptions*.

- Are you always ready to jump in with your own ideas as soon as the other person pauses? ☐

- If the other person starts saying something you disagree with, do you interrupt to put your point of view? ☐

- If you can guess the end of a person's sentence, do you complete it for them? ☐

- If so, do you then continue talking yourself? ☐

- Do you try to stop them if you feel the other person is getting angry or upset? ☐

Decide which is your worst weakness and try making a conscious effort to overcome it. (Men, by and large, need to make a particular effort not to interrupt women: and women need to be assertive enough not to let themselves be ignored by men.)

Giving feedback

Now let's look at a more positive aspect. To be an active listener, you need to give appropriate *feedback* to the person who is talking. That is, you need to *let them know* that you are paying attention and trying to understand things from their point of view. There are many more ways of doing this than most people imagine.

Which of the following forms of feedback might be appropriate in any of the listening you need to do in small groups?

- Reflecting back what the other person seems to be saying by restating it in my own words ☐

- Asking them to say more about things I don't follow ☐

- Happily tolerating pauses, which may encourage the talker to carry on and dig deeper ☐

- Offering my own opinions or solutions ☐

- Refraining from offering my own opinions or solutions ☐

- Using non-verbal noises (e.g. 'Mmm' and 'Uh-huh') ☐

- Using body language (e.g. eye contact, facial expressions, different body postures) ☐

- Responding to *their* non-verbal noises or body language (especially if they seem anxious or angry), e.g. by encouraging or calming them ☐

- Summarizing key points they have made ☐

Clearly, different group situations – e.g. tutorials, seminars, practical work with a couple of colleagues, informal conversations, etc. – will call for different kinds of feedback. Although computer conferencing group-work (which I mentioned a page or two back) does not involve you in listening, it does demand that students give one another (written) feedback; otherwise people soon stop sending in messages. I leave you to decide which kinds of feedback you are already good at giving and which kinds you might want to improve in.

In thinking how to get best value out of group discussion, the same principles apply as with any other learning situation. Prepare for it beforehand, participate actively during it, and reflect on it afterwards. This applies as much to online computer groups as it does to groups meeting face-to-face.

Preparing for group discussion

How you might best prepare for group discussion depends on what form the group will take. Usually, however, I imagine you should be able to:

● Find out what kind of group will operate (e.g. 'as normal'?)

● Find out whether your participation will be *assessed*

● Find out what topic is to be discussed

● Do any reading or practical work that has been suggested as preparation for the discussion

● Have informal chats with one or two members of the group, in advance, if you are especially concerned about anything

● Write down one or two points – e.g. a question, a particular piece of evidence, a relevant personal experience – that you would like to mention in the discussion

● Consider what you might hope to gain from the group session

● And *if you are* to *present a paper for discussion*:

  - Make sure you know how long you have to speak

  - Check whether anyone else is to make a presentation and, if so, on what aspect of the topic and whether they'll speak before or after you

  - Research your paper thoroughly

  - But don't try to cram in all you've learned – two or three main points are probably all you'll have time to do justice to

  - Give your paper a clear introduction, middle and conclusion (ending perhaps with a question you'd like to hear the group give their comments on)

- Consider whether you might want to give group members a handout or use a chalkboard, flipchart, overhead projector or computer presentation

- Write out your paper

- Rehearse reading it (or speaking from notes based on it)

- Cut it, if necessary, to a length that can be expected to hold the group's attention (perhaps fifteen minutes maximum)

Have you presented a discussion paper yourself, or listened to colleagues presenting one? If so, which of the above suggestions about preparing a paper do you think people seem most often to neglect?

My own impression is that discussion papers are spoiled most often by the speaker trying to cram too much in. He or she therefore speaks much too fast for the group to follow and/or runs on so long that they get impatient and lose interest. You may have observed other faults. (The equivalent fault in computer conferencing is to give colleagues too many screenfuls of text to read.)

Participating in group discussion

It should be clear from what I've said so far in this chapter that 'participating' does not mean talking as much as possible – not even if you are presenting a paper. Ideally, you should have brought one or two points of your own that you'd like to contribute to the discussion. And yet more points may occur to you as you hear other people's arguments. So you should have something to talk about.

However, you should still be participating even when you are not offering views of your own. This you will do by listening actively and giving feedback to other speakers.

Expressing your own ideas

You can get a lot of credit from the rest of the group by being a thoughtful responder to other people's contributions. Everybody appreciates a good listener. But, to get proper benefit from the group situation, you really need to put some of your own thoughts and feelings out into the open. You won't learn as much as you might unless you get some feedback from the group yourself.

Some students do find this difficult, especially when the group is new and they are worrying about whether the tutor or other group members will think them ignorant. Unfortunately, not talking can create a similar impression, or even one of lack of interest. (In computer conferencing, group members who read other people's messages, but never respond or send any of their own, are known as 'lurkers'.)

If non-talking is a problem for you, you may find it evaporates once you get used to the group. One way of speeding up this process is to chat with individual members of the group away from the formal discussion sessions. You may also want to mention your difficulty to the leader of your group, if there is one. If the leader is aware that you do want to make a contribution, she or he may be able to find a way of helping you get started.

Of course, you may have the reverse problem. You may be the sort of talkative person who dominates the discussion and makes the reticent members even more hesitant about joining in. If so, I think I've already hinted at what you might do about it. Try listening more, encouraging other people to speak, and giving feedback. Whenever you do speak, keep to the point and be as succinct as possible. If your colleagues want you to elaborate, they'll ask you.

Making notes

Making notes during small-group sessions is often quite difficult. But it would be a pity to lose the kinds of valuable insight that are liable to come up. Keep paper and pencil to hand and be prepared to make occasional jottings. Many students find that 'spray diagrams' or 'ideas maps' (see Chapter 9) are a convenient way of doing this. Others simply make a *list* of points worth thinking more about.

Reflecting on the group session

As with any learning experience, a group session will lose most of its value unless you reflect on it afterwards. Writing some notes will be one aid in doing this. Think back over what was helpful, unhelpful or just unexpected about the session. Did you get what you were hoping for? Did you get something else as well (or instead)? If you presented a paper, what sort of feedback did you get? How might you do it differently another time? If someone else gave a paper, what did you learn from their presentation? How would you rate the quality of your listening, talking and giving of feedback? Is there any follow-up work you need to do?

Reflecting on how the group operates

Apart from aspects of the topic that still bother you, you and your colleagues might want to talk about *how the group operates* and whether this might be improved. Few groups of any sort (and here I can think of certain university committees I've been on) spend as much time as they should on this.

Which of the following questions, for example, do you think members might usefully consider in the kind of learning groups you have been a member of?

- Is the group about the right size? ☐
- Does it meet about as often as it should? ☐
- Are the physical surroundings conducive to good discussion? ☐
- Does the tutor take an appropriate role, e.g. neither leaving you to flounder nor ruling with a rod of iron? ☐
- Are the topics well chosen? ☐
- Are the group activities appropriate? ☐
- Do members prepare adequately for the sessions? ☐
- Do members get satisfactory learning from the group? ☐
- Does the group contain non-talkers or over-talkers? ☐
- Do members listen actively and give good feedback? ☐
- Are there any serious conflicts between group members? ☐

What if you and your colleagues identify any constant problems that seem to be interfering with the group as a learning situation? You may want to discuss them with the tutor or leader (if there is one) and/or ask the group to address them as a topic for discussion.

Tutorless groups

The reduced funding of colleges may mean that each tutor is now allocated too many students for them to be able to work with you in small groups as often as you and your colleagues would like, therefore consider organizing your own. Tutors do not have to be present in order for learning to take place. Provided students are prepared to take the meetings seriously – preparing for them properly and applying the kinds of listening skill we've been talking about above – they can manage perfectly well on a do-it-yourself basis. If you are part of a self-help group, then you may be doing this anyway.

Of course, students can also learn from each other in more casual circumstances. Useful discussions often spring up in labs and studios, in common rooms and pubs, on computer networks and on the bus going home. Even though you will not have prepared for such discussions, you should always be ready to participate as actively as possible, to reflect on anything useful that emerges and, if necessary, jot something down in your notebook.

And don't forget that students can learn from one another in groups of *two* as well as in larger gatherings. You will soon become aware of colleagues who have a deeper understanding of a particular topic than you have, and from whom you can occasionally seek discussion and advice. Similarly, you should be prepared to give some of your time to advising colleagues in those areas you are best at – not just out of natural kindness but also because the effort of sharing experience with someone else helps you get your own ideas sorted out.

Listen with special attention to people whose views you disagree with. They can often do more than anyone to help you clarify your own.

Follow-up activities

1 Try applying this chapter's ideas about 'learning-from-listening' to some lecture whose topic is not especially interesting to you. Does this approach enable you to get anything more from the lecture than you would otherwise have expected to?

2 In particular, team up with one or two other students to compare notes about a lecture and what you've got from it. If this works for you, consider doing it regularly.

3 Using the list on page 130, consider what kind of feedback is being given by people in discussion groups and conversations, and practise giving whatever kind you regard as appropriate when you can.

4 Use the ideas in this chapter to prepare for, and contribute to, your next discussion group. Did you get any more from the discussion than you would normally expect to? Did you put more into the discussion than you normally would?

5 Get together with colleagues to discuss how your 'learning-from-listening' situations (especially lectures and small-group work) might be made more rewarding.

8
Learning from materials

'At first I thought it was just a cop-out on the part of the lecturers – giving us all this stuff to work through so as they could get on with their research. But I've come to find I enjoy working on my own, or with my small group [two other students], with well-structured materials, and I reckon I get more individual help from my tutor than I do on ordinary courses.'

One of the big changes in post-secondary education over the last few years has been the swing towards what I call materials-based learning. Whether on campus or at a distance, students are spending much less time in class. Instead, they are spending much more time learning on their own with the help of specially-prepared materials – e.g. study guides, sets of journal articles, workbooks, audio- and video-tapes, CD-ROMs – or with materials they find for themselves (with advice from tutors) in libraries or on the Internet.

Forms of materials-based learning

Such guided 'self-teaching' takes a number of different forms and goes by many different names, some of which are listed below. Which of the following types of learning have you already been involved with or think you might be soon?

- open learning ☐
- distance learning ☐
- flexible learning ☐

- independent learning ☐
- supported self-study ☐
- self-managed learning ☐
- computer-assisted learning ☐
- technology-based teaching ☐
- flexi-study ☐
- resource-based learning ☐

If you haven't got involved with any of these just yet, I'm sure you eventually will. It seems to be the way higher education is going – largely as a means of coping with hugely increasing numbers of students without a similar increase in staff and funding.

So, many students are having to take more responsibility than ever for their own learning. They may be working on campus at a college or, as 'distance learners', in their homes or workplaces. They may be spending just a few hours on a collection of learning materials as *part* of a course or several months on a fully materials-based course. They may be meeting regularly with other learners and a tutor, or they may never set eyes on them. Their learning programme may include a certain amount of face-to-face contact; but it may include none at all. And they may or may not be doing other kinds of courses alongside, or in between, their materials-based activities.

Materials-based learning was pioneered in the 1970s by UK institutions like the Open University and National Extension College which cater for distance learners. Since then, many other colleges have adapted it for at least some of their courses – sometimes for distance learners, sometimes for students who spend much of their time on campus. It is also widely used in the on-job training of civil servants, hotel workers, police officers, doctors, engineers and practically any vocational group you can think of.

So what sort of materials might you be learning from? Here is a selection. Which of them have you already used or might expect to soon?

- textbooks ☐
- collections of articles ☐
- other printed material ☐
- study guides/course guides ☐
- workbooks ☐
- practical kits ☐
- audio-tapes ☐
- video-tapes ☐
- computer-driven resources (e.g. CAL or multimedia) ☐

Printed materials

Students have always spent most of their study time with books and other printed materials. But materials-based teaching has found some new uses for print. What forms might you be using?

Textbooks and articles

You will almost certainly have used textbooks and possibly collections of articles (or 'readers' as they are sometimes called). One or more such books is often required reading for each course. You may be expected to buy such books yourself or they may be provided for you out of your course fee. Chapters 5 and 6 in this book are especially concerned with how to get the most out of such material.

Other printed material

Some materials-based courses also include printed materials that were not written with students especially in mind, e.g. reference works, pamphlets, newspaper extracts, maps, etc. For instance, the resource materials for a course on disease in cattle may contain a standard reference manual, statistical summaries, photographs, newspaper articles, and leaflets issued by government departments concerned with food and agriculture.

Study guides

A study guide (or sometimes 'course guide') is a booklet that your tutors will have written specially to guide you through your course. In this it differs from a textbook which the author will have written without any particular course in mind.

The purpose of the study guide is to make sure you know how the course works and to guide you in the various activities that you will be carrying out as part of that course. Thus it may contain:

- An outline of the course – its content and week-by-week timetable

- Learning objectives – what you are expected to be able to *do* or do better by the time you have completed the course

- Detailed notes about the course materials (books, pamphlets, CD-ROMs, or whatever) and what part each is meant to play

- Advice on how to use the materials

- Activities that you are expected to carry out, on your own or with a group, using the materials

- Instructions for practical work, guidance about safety, security, how to get technical help, and so on

- Comments from your teacher that 'top and tail' each phase of your work with the materials, e.g. introducing each new topic, giving clearer explanations or better examples of points that are not made well enough in the materials, providing summaries of the key ideas

- Self-test questions enabling you to check how well you have mastered the objectives for each phase of the course

- Course work assignments to be graded and/or commented on by tutors

- Details of how your work will be assessed.

Workbooks

Most open learners do most of their learning from specially prepared workbooks. A workbook is like a study guide only more so. It will contain everything a study guide contains plus a lot more besides.

In particular, workbooks will probably contain much more *teaching* – so much, in fact, that you may not have much need for textbooks on the course. Indeed, it may be the lack of a suitable textbook that has prompted your teachers to write the workbooks instead.

Workbooks are exactly what the name suggests – books that you work with. But they are also books that you work *in*. Usually they will use A4 format and leave wide margins and plenty of other space on the pages for you to write down your own ideas. They will probably have frequent questions or tasks (often called 'activities') for you to carry out – just as this book does. Such activities will then be followed by 'feedback' which helps you check your response to the activity or just think some more about it. Workbooks are also likely to be more user-friendly than most textbooks. They are often written in conversational style and address the reader as 'you' (again like this book).

What *benefits* might you expect if you were getting most of your teaching from printed materials – rather than in classroom sessions (or other media)? And what might you feel you were *missing*?

There are all sorts of benefits you may have mentioned – e.g. you can learn when and where you choose, you can carry printed materials around easily, you don't need to buy or rent any special viewing equipment, you may get frequent checks on how much or how well you are learning and the teaching is always there for you to refer back to whenever you need.

On the negative side, you might feel you could miss the stimulus of hearing your teachers talk, seeing their minds at work, weighing up what they think of as important or less important in the subject, getting updated on topical developments, working collaboratively with your fellow-students, using other media like video and computers, and so on.

Audio and video materials

Audio- and video-tapes play a vital role in some materials-based courses, usually along with printed materials that help you use them to maximum effect.

Audio-tapes

Sound can be a very effective medium in materials-based learning. In the early years of the Open University, radio was the chief means of delivering it. Nowadays, however, we make far more use of the audio-cassette. This is because the audio-cassette is much more user-friendly. You don't have to be sitting by your radio at fixed times; you can listen whenever it suits you.

And there are more advantages. You don't need to just sit and listen to the teacher who is talking to you on the tape. Right at your finger-tips you have a stop or pause switch – and a rewind switch. So you can make your teacher shut up if you want to think for a minute or two (or pour a cup of coffee). And you can make them repeat what they've said as often as you need to hear it – until you are sure you understand. How often can students do this to their teacher in a conventional classroom?

There are three main ways of using audio in materials-based teaching:

- *Just listening.* Talks, discussions, interviews, acted scenes, natural sounds – stuff you can learn from even when your eyes and hands are busy with other things, e.g. while driving a car or washing the dishes.

- *Listening and looking.* Here you have to use your eyes as well as your ears. You get printed material (or physical objects) to look at along with the audio-tape. The accompanying print may contain diagrams, photographs, maps, charts, tables of figures, etc. which the audio will talk you through.

- *Listening, looking and doing.* Sometimes the audio-teacher may ask you to stop the tape and write something in your workbook, or carry out some practical work with materials and equipment, or with other people. When you switch on again the teacher will comment on what you've done.

But what's so special about audio-teaching? Think of the subjects you are interested in. Or think what you might expect from me if I'd provided an audio-cassette to go with this book. What might you hope to get from audio that you couldn't get so easily from printed materials?

If, for example, you are studying languages, the benefits of hearing native speakers on tape will be obvious to you. But audio can play a role in practically any subject area. For example, an audio-tape can help you make best use of your time by giving you a means of learning while doing other things, e.g. driving a car or doing the ironing. Again, an audio-tape can talk you through tasks like studying a map or a table of figures – where you might find it distracting to have to keep turning aside to look at printed guidance. Not least of its benefits, though, is that it can be used to make the materials-based teaching more human and personal.

Students generally speak well of audio-teaching – especially when the audio-tape is linked with workbooks or other printed material. Here is what some have told me:

- *'It's like having your tutor in the room with you.'*

- *'I get more sense out of the books now because I can hear the author's voice in my mind as I read.'*

- *'The tapes are alive – they've got warmth and personality – and they cheer me up when the bookwork is getting a bit much.'*

Video-tapes

You may find yourself watching television as part of your materials-based learning. If you are doing an Open University undergraduate course, the material may be broadcast to you by the BBC. But with many Open University courses, and most courses from other colleges that use television, the material will come on video-tape. In the same way as audio-cassettes, videos are more user-friendly – provided, of course, you've got easy access to a playback machine.

Video adds an extra dimension to learning. You can have pictures in workbooks together with sound from an audio-tape. But a video brings you *moving* pictures (and in full colour). And the sound – which may be people talking or music or voice-over commentary – ties in with those moving pictures to give you a sense of 'being there' that is difficult for other media to match.

If you are unlucky, the videos you see may be simply recorded lectures. And 'talking heads' can be pretty dreary. But video (like audio) can be used to engage you in learning of a kind that books and classroom teaching cannot match. For example, videos may:

- show you how to use tools or equipment or demonstrate skills that you may be learning – e.g. interviewing or picture-restoring.

- help you analyse change over time, using animation, freeze-frame, slow-motion or speeded-up pictures – e.g. the movements of an animal or the growth of a plant.

- take you into situations – e.g. into an intensive care unit or the cockpit of an aircraft about to land – which you might not otherwise be able to enter.

- provide source material for you to explore or analyse, using principles or techniques taught in the course – e.g. film of children at play or of scenes of violence at a football match.

As with audio-tapes, you would normally have study guides or workbooks to help you get the most out of videos like these.

Practical work materials

If you are learning practical skills you may well need to practise with equipment or materials. You may be able to do this in a college laboratory or a company's workshops. Even so, your tutors may sometimes provide all the necessary materials in a practical kit you can use on your own or with colleagues. The Open University's distance learners know these as 'home experiment kits'. For instance, a helium neon-laser for producing holograms was necessary in one course I remember. Other practical kits I remember have included items like rock specimens, refrigeration piping, an electronic keyboard and even a robot. (Not all in the same kit, of course!)

Needless to say, the practical kits won't help you much on their own. You need guidance on what to do with them. You'll normally get this from a printed workbook or study guide, but sometimes you may get an audio- or video-cassette to take you through the practical work.

Thinking about video and practical kits now as well as audio, can you identify any further *benefits* you might get from such materials in the subjects you are studying? And can you foresee any *problems* you might have in learning from them?

You may feel that, like audio, video can enhance the learning of any subject, if only by offering a bit of variety. But you may have gone beyond this and thought of things you would like to hear and see that such materials might provide, e.g. interviews with famous names in your subject, performances of plays or music, filmed highlights of field trips.

What about practical kits? Obvious uses perhaps if you are studying in the area of mathematics, science or technology; but even in arts and social sciences courses you may have seen some scope.

As for problems in learning from such materials, much depends on the help you get from a study guide. Take audio and video, for example. Most of us tend to half-listen to radio and watch television with half an eye while relaxing with our feet up and a drink at our elbow. Using such media for serious study is quite different and usually needs to be learned. You could expect a course guide or workbook to help you by suggesting what to listen or look for and setting activities that would improve your understanding of the key points.

You may also think you'd find this form of study rather dull unless you have someone with whom you can discuss what you are learning. As with all materials-based learning, you'll get more out of it if you can work on your tapes or practical kit with one or more other students or at least discuss your findings with an interested friend or partner.

Computer-based resources

For hundreds of years, students have managed perfectly well without computers and most still do. But more and more students – in arts and social science subjects as well as mathematics, science and technology – are beginning to find them extremely useful, and often essential. And I am not talking merely about courses about computers and computing, where it would be very difficult to learn *without* using computers. The use of computers is much more widespread.

Why is this? What is the attraction? Computers mean different things to students in different subject areas; but the benefits they gain fall into two main categories:

- being able to carry out the old study tasks more efficiently; and

- being able to learn in ways that were not previously possible at all.

In which of the following ways have you already used computers (even if it was not as part of your studies)?

- Word processing ☐
- Developing and filing your notes ☐
- Calculating ☐
- Using spreadsheets ☐
- Producing tables, graphs, diagrams and other graphics ☐
- Using spreadsheets ☐
- Using databases (on hard disk or CD-ROM) ☐
- Computer-assisted learning (CAL or CBT) ☐
- Interactive multimedia ☐
- Internet (and the World Wide Web) ☐
- Email ☐
- Computer conferencing ☐

New ways with old tasks

The first seven items in the list above are new and less laborious ways of carrying out old tasks. And they aren't confined to materials-based learning; these tools can be used by students on practically *any* kind of course. As one mature student told me:

> *'I have spent much of my life in the last 15 years writing. As a result of the new technology I now do it quite differently in a host of ways which I only partly understand – how I assemble and organise ideas, how I organise the work over time, how I work with other people, how I draft and redraft material. These are important skills which a growing number of people will need in the future if they are to survive in the workplace.'*

Many students, for instance, have greatly improved their efficiency by learning how to use word processing. The ability to make changes to what you have written, to delete bits you don't like, pick up a paragraph from page 3 and move it back to page 1, insert headings, and so on – without having to tear up everything you've done and start over again (or settle for making do with something that you know you could improve) – can transform the way you think and create. You can be much more flexible and inventive; you can try things out; see how they look and, if you don't like them, delete them (or move them to another part of the document you are writing).

Added to which, you can draw and insert diagrams or charts, use the software's spelling and grammar checkers to alert you to errors you may have committed in your creative fury and, finally, print out a report or essay whose smart appearance will outshine even your best handwriting.

Similarly, if your subject involves much number-crunching, computer software can save you hours of mental arithmetic or prodding away at a pocket calculator. This can free you to concentrate on what the calculations are about, and what the results might mean, rather than getting lost in the mechanics of cranking it out or detecting where you've gone wrong. And if you need to plough your way through dozens of journals looking for obscure references or track down the patterns in decades of social statistics, then a computerised database may save you hours of legwork and/or labour and also help you summarize your findings in elegant tables and charts.

There are snags, of course. You'll lose a certain amount of study time in learning how to use the software (though you'll more than make up for it later). You may also want to invest more of your time in learning how to type properly. (Though many productive writers, including me and my wife who has published seven novels, still find that two fingers on each hand are quite enough to keep up with the speed at which we can think!)

The power of the technology and the glossy appearance of what it produces can also lull one into a false sense of security or tempt one into doing things that are better not done on a computer. People can use word processors to produce gorgeous-looking documents that contain utter drivel or are poorly expressed. And just because a computer enables you to do certain things is no indication that you'd necessarily find it useful to do them. For instance, you could write up all your notes on the computer and file them systematically for easy access. But you may decide this is more trouble than it is worth and that, anyway, you'd rather keep your notes on each topic as paper copies (along with photocopied material, sketches, press cuttings, etc.) rather than store them on the computer.

New ways of learning

The final five items in the list above go beyond doing old tasks more efficiently. They are new ways of learning that have been made possible by computers.

Computer-assisted learning (CAL)

You may also come across this use of computers described as CBL (computer-based learning) or as CBT (computer-based training). If you've spent any time at all learning how to use computer software, you may well have learned some of it from a computer-based tutorial package. But CAL packages are available in a wide range of other subjects – e.g. engineering design, family history, philosophy. (I have just been sent details of a new CAL package on essay writing.) The computer will often enable you to do things faster, or more realistically or with greater understanding than other methods will allow – and even things that would be *impossible* using other methods. How so?

The computer's power to teach lies chiefly in its ability to:

● store a huge amount of information;

● select from it at great speed;

● present it in a variety of forms (e.g. text, moving pictures, sound); and

● respond differently according to the different requests or answers it gets from different students.

What this means is that the computer can show you different material according to what *you* type on the computer keyboard or indicate with your mouse. For instance, you can tell the computer what you would like to see next. Or you can ask it to alter diagrams or tables of figures on the screen. Similarly, if you make mistakes in answering questions the computer has put to you, it will be able to tell you immediately where you have gone wrong. So you can *interact* with the material in a way that you can't with a book or even (as often as you might like) with a human tutor.

Two of the main styles of computer teaching are:

1 Tuition

Here the teaching package requires the computer to act as a patient tutor or coach. It leads you through a sequence of material which you are expected to master. The computer can discover in what areas each student has difficulties – then explain the ideas involved, using appropriate examples and exercises – and test you at each step to check how well you have understood.

Different students may be presented with different examples and test exercises, according to their earlier responses. And the program may 'branch' different students into different kinds of teaching according to the particular difficulties or interests they reveal.

2 Simulation

The second form of computer teaching uses the computer to model or simulate a particular situation or system with which you can interact. Thus you might be able to 'experiment' in total safety with, let's say, a nuclear reactor, an ailing hospital patient, the processes of geological change, or the economic structure of the EEC.

You can call up the information that will enable you to run the reactor, treat the patient, and so on, as you think fit, trying out your interpretation of the underlying principles. The computer will show or tell you what effects your decisions are having – especially if the reactor is about to blow up or the patient die on you.

Interactive multimedia

Multimedia is computer-assisted learning at its most adventurous. It can build in the benefits of a variety of media – print, audio, photographs, animation, moving film (all in full colour, of course) – as well as enabling you to interact with the teaching as described above and, in some cases, draw in relevant information from the Internet. You will often be encouraged to explore your own routes through the material to suit your personal interests, allowing you a freedom that is impossible in classroom teaching. The teaching package may be made available to you from a central computer on your college campus, on a floppy disk, on a CD-ROM or you may reach it via the Internet.

If you've already used some form of computer-assisted learning, what do you like best and least about it? If you haven't, how do you feel about the idea of using it?

Many students find it easier to concentrate with computers than they do with workbooks and other media. And they appreciate getting a kind of interactive feedback that other media cannot give. But there is the snag that you may not be able to work on the package at a time and place to suit yourself as perhaps you can with other media. And some CAL packages are tedious and not very interactive – so what they give could be obtained more easily from a book.

The best computer-assisted learning packages are excellent – they will challenge you, encourage your creativity and engage you in deep level learning. The worst (and, of course, they are easier and cheaper to develop) can be awful – they will bore you, frustrate you, make you feel controlled by the machine and leave you nothing to do but tedious surface-level learning. Keep critical about whatever CAL packages you come across and don't waste more of your study time than you need to on poor ones. (This goes for all materials, of course – books, audio-tapes, videos, etc., as well as computer materials.)

Electronic mail (Email)

Electronic mail is a system that enables you to use a computer to send a written message to one or more people, e.g. your tutor or other students. They will see your message next time they 'log on' to their computer and can choose whether to reply then or later (or not at all). You may also be able to attach bulky documents (e.g. essays) to your message or even spreadsheets, software and audio or video material. Or, of course, you may have such items sent to you.

On a materials-based course, or on any course where you don't often see your tutor (or even your fellow students), email can be a useful way of keeping in touch and of getting help if you run into difficulties. It offers a new way of running a self-help group. (For details of academic 'discussion lists' using email, see *Mailbase* and *Tile.Net* in 'References'.)

If you are studying on campus, you will probably be able to send email (and perhaps do computer conferencing and get into the Internet) free of charge through any computer on your college network. If you are a distance learner you will need your own computer and software, together with a telephone line and a device called a modem which links your computer with the telephone system. And you will have a bigger phone bill to pay!

Computer conferencing

This is a development of email in which tutors and groups of students can send messages for the whole group to read, enabling them to discuss the ideas in their course. As with email, participants will not usually be 'on line' all at the same time. You can send and read messages whenever it suits you. Unlike many face-to-face meetings, everyone can say their piece and can reflect for as long as they like before responding to another person's contribution.

In a course where face-to-face meetings are rare, computer conferencing can be invaluable – provided it is well run by your tutor. For instance, you can share ideas with other students, get feedback from them and collaborate with them on projects in small groups. What students have to say about the subject matter often becomes part of the course content – because it leads to further questions and discussion from which others can learn. When the students are professionals, with relevant experiences and viewpoints to relate – e.g. nurses, managers or engineers – the tutor may learn from them too.

Much does depend on the skill and vigilance of the tutor who is running (or 'moderating') the conference. He or she needs, for example, to ensure everyone is competent with the conferencing software, make clear the ground rules, set up a worthwhile sequence of discussion topics and activities, split the class into workable sub-groups, encourage students to contribute, intervene in the discussion where necessary to correct any misinformed or misleading messages and to raise new issues or pick out some key points from what people have been saying so far. Without a skilled moderator, conferences can quickly fizzle out.

Internet (and the World Wide Web)

The Internet is a means of using a computer to obtain information from millions of other computers around the world. It is also a way of sending email and joining online discussion groups (like computer conferencing), but its special feature is the World Wide Web – a facility that gives you access to huge amounts of downloadable information, e.g. text, graphics, audio, video, software. This covers practically every imaginable subject and is provided by libraries, museums, governments, companies, universities, research organizations and many other institutions and individuals.

Even if you are studying on campus, your college may put materials on the Web, or on its internal network ('intranet'), for you to consult or download. But many colleges are now offering complete materials-based *courses* on the Internet – and their students may be studying in any country in the world. (See *Spectrum* and *World Lecture Hall* in 'References'.)

The World Wide Web (WWW) has tremendous potential for students – a world of information, literally at your fingertips. But information is not the same as knowledge, let alone wisdom. There is a lot of valuable stuff out there, but there is also a lot of rubbish (even though it may look very authoritative on your screen). So, as always, keep up your critical, questioning approach. Who was responsible for putting up the information? Why should you trust them? Does what they say seem accurate, unbiased and up-to-date? How does it compare with your own experience and what you have learned elsewhere?

'Surfing the Web' can also be very costly – in time even if you are not paying for the calls – because it can take much longer than you think to find and download the material. Think of it like going into the largest library in the universe where new 'books' are pouring in by the minute; but you can't easily browse among them; no one has made decisions about whether they are worth stocking; they aren't classified; there isn't a catalogue; and there's no friendly librarian standing by to advise you. Little wonder you can easily get distracted, lose sight of your study purpose and end up swamped by a deluge of information. It helps to have a very clear idea as to what you are looking for.

So, computers can be a useful or even essential aid to your learning. Many students, I find, are still anxious about them. (Tutors too!) Well, computers won't bite and you can't break them, and there is a lot to learn if you are to get the best out of them. Apart from learning how to make the computer and software do what you want it to, you may also need to learn a new set of study skills for finding and making sense of ideas that are coming to you in forms and quantities that you have never previously experienced. I know what it's like because I too am still struggling to understand how best to *teach* with computers. To do this I first need experience of learning with them. Coming to grips with the new technology makes students of us all!

With any materials-based learning resources – but especially when using computers, which often seem to mesmerize us into losing sight of the passing hours – it is vital to keep asking: 'Is this the best way I could be using my study time?' Sometimes it won't be. Give every item of likely material a fair trial but be prepared to find that some recommended CD-ROMs or videos or even chapters of a textbook do not really suit your study purposes. Whenever you decide this is so, cut your losses, and move on to something more worthwhile.

The need for human support

So what is materials-based learning like to work with? Clearly it suits some students more than others. Some distance learners actually choose it because they can't easily attend classes, or because they don't like learning in groups. Many on-campus students are rather suspicious of it at first but come to find it suits them very well. They feel more in control of the course and how, where and when they study it. Yet others still echo what this on-campus student told me:

> *'I've enjoyed the course and I know I've got as much out of it as any other I've taken. I'd certainly consider doing another materials-based course but I wouldn't want all my courses to be like this. There's just not enough contact with other people for my liking.'*

How much human contact do you need? There's a great deal you can learn from well-structured learning materials. But some students don't take easily to working on their own without the feedback from other people that they are used to. They may find it difficult to concentrate and start losing their motivation. Some distance learners in particular may have to fight this, but as we've seen in the quote above, on-campus students may be affected too. However, even students on *lecture*-based courses are nowadays being heard to complain about the lack of human contact. I heard this comment from a student who had previously done some Open University courses but was now studying at a traditional university:

> *'Now I'm in my third year, I only get to see my tutors on Friday mornings. It's like doing a distance learning course – but without the distance learning materials!'*

But however excellent your learning materials, you'll learn yet more if you can get support from some real live human beings. However good it is, the materials contain only pre-recorded teaching. They have to do all things for all students. They can't do much to respond to your individual needs. They can't answer your questions. They may not be able to give you yet another explanation when you still don't understand. They can't look over your shoulder while you make your first attempt at some tricky practical task. They can't cheer you up when you feel you are not learning as fast as you want to. These are things that can be done only by other people.

There are many ways in which students on materials-based courses might hope to get support from other people. Which of the following do you enjoy already (or might try to get more of) on your courses?

At a distance

- Helpful written comments on your course work from your tutor ☐

- Telephone conversations between you and your tutor ☐

- Telephone conversations between you and another student ☐

- You and several other students in telephone contact at the same time, with or without a tutor, by means of a 'conference call' ☐

- Video conferencing (enabling you to see as well as hear the others) ☐

- Email contact with your tutor and other students ☐

- Computer conferencing ☐

Face-to-face

- Sessions in which your tutor goes over your course work with you ☐

- Meeting frequently with a group of fellow-students to work on a common task ☐

- Student self-help groups meeting occasionally throughout the course ☐

- Occasional 'surgeries', seminars, tutorials, lectures by tutors ☐

- One-day, one-week, weekend, or other short group sessions (residential or otherwise) ☐

- Help from librarians or technicians or (if you are working) from your line manager or a mentor ☐

> **Materials-based learning can be enjoyable and effective. But for maximum effect you need appropriate support from other people. Make sure you get what you are entitled to – and provide what you can to fellow-students.**

Follow-up activities

1 If you are doing a materials-based course, consider how the chapters in this book might help you get more out of it.

2 Are you using the materials to best advantage? It might be worth comparing study methods with some fellow-students to find out whether you can learn from one another's approaches.

3 If you are not yet doing materials-based learning, find out whether you will be expected to do so, or have a choice of doing so, in the near future.

4 If you do find out what is likely to be involved, then talk to students who've done materials-based courses, ask to look at their course materials, find out what they can tell you about how best to learn from such teaching, etc.

5 If not, find out whether there are any materials you can easily get hold of that might help you with your studies anyway; for example many students on 'conventional' courses have made profitable use of Open University materials that are available in most college and many public libraries, or, if you have Internet access, try the World Wide Web.

9

Making and using notes

'What I'm doing with this book is I'm making a fairly detailed outline of each chapter. It's really the core of the course, and all the lectures relate to it, week by week. So I really have to have the whole structure of the author's thinking quite clear in my own head. But these others . . . well, I'm pretty familiar with the main ideas in these books already. So all I'm looking for is points where they differ from one another, or from my main text – and for interesting examples, so my notes are much briefer, just jottings about interesting points, and questions I have about them, references to other stuff I might want to chase up, that sort of thing.'

Most students spend a lot of their time making notes. Why do they do it? What form do their notes take? How do they store them? What use do they make of them afterwards? Are they always worth the paper they are written on? These are the kinds of question that will underlie this chapter.

Why make notes?

Why do you write notes at all? Jot down in your notebook the first three reasons that come to mind.

Possible purposes

Here are some answers given to the above question by a number of students. Tick any you've not mentioned that you feel also apply to you:

1 'To help me understand what I'm hearing or reading about while I am studying it.' ☐

2 'To ensure I keep paying attention.' ☐

3 'To help me review the learning session afterwards.' ☐

4 'To ensure I have as full a statement as possible of what was actually said.' ☐

5 'To record my own thoughts or examples concerning what is being said.' ☐

6 'To remind myself of follow-up reading, etc.' ☐

7 'To have material to revise for exams.' ☐

8 'To sort out my own ideas on a topic.' ☐

9 'To plan my work for an assignment or in an exam.' ☐

As with all aspects of studying, the most appropriate way of making notes depends on your purpose. So, it is useful to be clear in your own mind about why you are making notes. Nine different purposes are mentioned above, and you may have written three completely different ones of your own.

Looking at the list above, I see an important distinction between purposes 1–7 and 8–9. They distinguish between the kind of notes you might write when:

a) you are trying to respond to *someone else's ideas* – e.g. from a lecture or a book

b) you are trying to produce and sort out *your own* ideas – e.g. in planning an assignment

Some people talk of (a) as 'taking' notes and (b) as 'making' notes. Unfortunately, this suggests that (a) is a passive process, rather like taking a recording. I believe it is more helpful to think of both as active, creative processes. For example, whatever notes you write about a book, you will be putting something of yourself into them. (Student 5 above seems to have this possibility in mind.) You can easily check how much of yourself you've put into your notes by seeing how differently a colleague will have written about the same book. You will have *made* something different of the book.

Possible benefits and problems

In both situations mentioned above, there are perhaps three main reasons for writing notes:

1 To aid concentration.

2 To help understanding and/or creativity.

3 To have some kind of record for future use.

All of these are *potential* benefits. But you don't get them automatically. You have to keep the purpose in mind and let it shape the sort of notes you are writing. For example:

Writing notes can keep you actively concentrating on what you are reading or hearing. *But*, in a lecture, you can become so concerned with noting what the lecturer has just said that you lose track of what she or he is saying now.

Writing notes can aid your understanding – but only if you *think* about the meaning of what you are reading or hearing. If you are simply trying (like student 4 above?) to get down a 'full statement', then you are probably restricting yourself to 'surface-level learning' (see Chapter 2). You may know what was said, but not know what it meant.

Writing notes can also provide a record for future use. But you need to know what sort of future use you have in mind – e.g. as a means of recalling the author's or lecturer's total argument, as a collection of choice examples to support an argument of your own, as guidance on further reading. Note how the student quoted at the beginning of this chapter explains the differences between her notes on different books. Notes you wrote with one future use in mind might not be helpful for certain other future uses.

A **Do you normally write notes with a view to using them again in the future?**

B **Do you actually make as much use of them in the future as you expected to at the time you wrote them? If not, why not?**

Many students report that they do not make as much use of their notes in the future as they expected to at the time they wrote them. They mention several reasons for this:

- they can't find the notes they need among all the other notes they've written before and since

- they can't read their own writing

- they can read it but they don't know what it means

- their ideas have developed so much since they wrote the notes that they now seem trivial or half-baked

- their notes are too sparse/too full/don't contain the kind of material they now need

This list, which no doubt you can add to, touches on several problems we'll be looking at in the rest of this chapter.

So there are several different purposes you might have in writing notes. And there are several reasons why your note-making might not be as helpful to you as you had hoped. Before we go on to consider what to do about this, let's give a moment's thought to some of the situations in which you might want to make notes.

When do you make notes?

Think about the following possible learning situations. How likely is it that you would normally be on the alert for points of interest to make notes about? Tick the appropriate box for Very Likely (VL), Possibly (P), or Most Unlikely (MU):

	VL	P	MU
1 Listening to one of a series of lectures from your regular tutors	☐	☐	☐
2 Listening to a presentation from a specially invited guest lecturer	☐	☐	☐
3 Observing some kind of practical demonstration	☐	☐	☐
4 Taking part in some sort of field work or carrying out practical (e.g. lab) work	☐	☐	☐

5 A group discussion session with a tutor ☐ ☐ ☐

6 Discussing the subject matter of your course with other students (and no tutor present) ☐ ☐ ☐

7 Conversations about your subject with people who are not taking the course (e.g. family) ☐ ☐ ☐

8 Reading books or other printed material that are 'set' or 'required' for your course ☐ ☐ ☐

9 Working on computer-based material ☐ ☐ ☐

10 Reading general background material that is not 'set' or 'required' ☐ ☐ ☐

11 Watching or listening to television and audio materials ☐ ☐ ☐

12 Leisure reading of newspapers and magazines and watching/listening to general television/radio programmes that may touch on your subject from time to time ☐ ☐ ☐

There are far more opportunities for making worthwhile notes than some students realize. For example, it escapes their attention (and therefore their notebooks) that practical work or some kind of experience 'in the field' (items 3 and 4 above) may raise points worth noting.'Likewise, many make notes only of what 'authority figures' (like lecturers and authors) have to say. It seems not to occur to them that their fellow-students (item 6) or even non-students (item 7) may make remarks (or stimulate thoughts of their own) that are worth making a note of.

The moral is to have a notebook and pencil within reach at all times. As I say in Chapter 10, 'Never let a good idea escape unrecorded' – whether it crops up in a seminar or a conversation in a pub, or even when you're relaxing with your feet up in front of the television.

Three ways of writing notes

There are many ways of writing notes. Which way you choose may vary with your subject, your purpose and your personal preference.

You may be simply jotting down isolated points that happen to interest you – which is what the student I quoted at the beginning of this chapter was describing in her second set of notes. These might consist simply of a list of examples, brief quotations, references, sketches and so on.

You may, on the other hand, be aiming to make a record of an author's or lecturer's complete line of argument or framework of ideas. This is what the student quoted was describing in her first set of notes. She needed to have a good grasp of the entire book because it was the core of her course. For this purpose, a more structured form of note-making seems necessary. There seem to be three basic approaches:

1 Straight prose summary.

2 Skeleton outline.

3 Patterned notes/spray diagram/spider chart.

These can no doubt be combined in several ways, and you may have developed quite different ways of your own. For example, in architecture or certain science subjects, many of your notes might take the form of sketches or diagrams with explanatory captions.

Comparing the three ways

Summary notes are a condensed version or précis of the original. They are usually written in continuous prose – more or less complete sentences and paragraphs. A *skeleton outline*, however, will make more use of single words and brief phrases and these will be set out as a list, using devices like headings and sub-headings, numbering, indentation, and so on.

The third form of notes goes by various names. Let's stick with *spray diagram* here. This also uses brief words and phrases, but the layout is quite different. You start off by naming the topic of your notes in the centre of a page. Then you spray out lines from the centre, one for each major branch of the topic and each labelled with a few words. Each branch can then be subdivided further by spraying off yet more lines from it, each one again carrying the appropriate (brief) label. And so on, until the topic runs out of subdivisions. Connections between one subdivision and another can be shown with linking lines.

Each of these ways of writing notes is illustrated on the next three pages. Each relates to the same chapter in this book, Chapter 6. (It doesn't matter whether or not you have read this chapter yourself yet.) Look at the three sets of notes and consider:

(a) From which set of notes can you most easily spot the *main points* of the chapter?

(b) Which notes most clearly show up the *relationships* between ideas in the chapter?

(c) Can you see a use in any of your study tasks for any of these forms of notes that you have *not* yet used?

(d) If you made notes on Chapter 6, how do yours differ from these? Do the differences reflect your purposes in writing them?

What did you think were the strengths and weaknesses of these ways of noting the main points of a book? Many students say that summaries are easy to write but awkward to use again later on. They find that skeleton outlines are better at showing up both the main ideas and the relationships between them. What do you think?

Spray diagrams get a mixed reception. Some students go overboard for them, noticing how usefully they can reveal the way topics split up into sub-topics and so on, and how the visual pattern (a different 'picture' for each page of notes) can help fix them in your mind. They also comment on how the limitations of space force you into using words and short phrases – thus making it less likely you will simply copy sentences from the author's text.

Other students complain that spray diagrams can't show the logical step-by-step structure of an argument. They also complain that they simply run out of space too quickly if they are trying to note material of any complexity – or else the page becomes too crowded and cramped to interpret later on. However, even some of those students admit that this may sometimes be a useful way of sorting out *your own* ideas as they occur to you, say, in planning an assignment. Some students write notes combining spray diagrams (to give an overview) with a summary to explain some of the details.

The Art of Reading Actively

Reading actively means reading questioningly + purposefully. Involves finding main ideas + important details + evaluating text.

Main ideas will be found at all levels from book as a whole to individual paragraphs. May detect the more general main ideas at Survey stage of SQ3R — more specific ones at Read stage. Look especially for topic sentence in paragraph (often 1st or last).

Students often don't distinguish between main ideas + important details — esp. if reading at surface level. (Can't see wood for trees.)

Important details clarify or support main ideas. (Which are important to me?)

Look out for author's visual + verbal signposts (emphasis, special phrases, etc). Don't overlook diagrams. Don't just skip difficulties — struggle on, re-read, discuss with other students/tutor.

Evaluate the text. Be critical. Ask questions to probe author's facts, opinions, evidence, argument, bias etc. And what have I learned from it? If necessary, make notes + discuss with other students.

Concentration is aided by seeking meaning (but see also Ch. 4). Don't sacrifice understanding for speed but vary speed according to purpose in reading.

Figure 3: Summary notes

The Art of Reading Actively

A. Active = purposeful, critical, questioning.
B. Look for <u>Main Ideas</u>
   1. Survey (SQ3R) for general ones (Ch.5)
   2. Read paragraphs for more specific ones
     a) Each para usually has one main idea.
     b) Usually in topic sentence (1st or last?)
C. Look for <u>Important Details</u>
   1. e.g. proof, example, support for main idea
   2. Usually at least one per main idea
   3. Which do I consider important?
D. In hunt for main idea and important details:
   1. Watch for signposts
     a) Visual (layout, etc)
     b) Verbal (clue words)
   2. Study diagrams, etc.
   3. Don't ignore difficulties
E. <u>Evaluate</u> the text
   1. Be sceptical (Expect the author to prove)
   2. Compare with my own experience
   3. What do I get from it?
   4. Discuss with other students
F. Make <u>Notes</u>:
   1. If I need them (for my purposes)
   2. At Recall stage (of SQ3R)
   3. Compare with other students'.
G. Concentrate:
   1. By seeking understanding (not memorisation)
   2. and see Chapter 4 hints.
H. Vary reading speed:
   1. according to purpose
   2. but not at expense of understanding.

Figure 4: Skeleton outline

The Art of Reading Actively

Figure 5: Spray diagram

Notes in different circumstances

How do your particular circumstances affect the notes you take? Of chief importance to mention here are: reading, lectures, discussion groups and sorting out your own ideas – e.g. for an assignment.

The main problem with notes is knowing what to put in and what to leave out. Working from books you get more time to make up your mind than you do in lectures or discussion groups. But this can be both a blessing and a curse. You need to steer a course between too much detail and too little. And how much is too much? This depends, as always, on *why* you are making the notes.

Notes from reading

Here are some suggestions for making notes from books and articles. Some of them will be familiar to you if you have already read Chapters 5 or 6. Tick those that seem applicable to *your* reading.

1 Survey the book/article to check whether or not it is likely to contain anything worth noting ☐

2 Decide whether you will be making notes on the whole thing or merely sections of it ☐

3 Decide whether you want a complete outline of the author's argument or whether you are merely hoping to pick up a few bits of information (e.g. to add to what you already know) ☐

4 Skim through each chosen chapter or section *before* you make notes so as to see the overall structure and identify some of the main ideas ☐

5 Read the material carefully, concentrating on what it *means* to you – not on what you are going to put in your notes ☐

6 Close the book, *recall* the main ideas and important details, and draft some notes ☐

7 Review the section and amend your notes if you feel you've missed anything of significance, *but*: ☐

   ● keep them *brief* – words and phrases rather than whole sentences (unless you need quotations) ☐

- make sure you use your *own words* (unless you need quotations) □

- distinguish in your notes between the author's ideas and ideas you have had while reading them □

The essence of effective note-making is selectivity. Many students seem to read with one finger tracing along the lines of their book while the other hand diligently copies down great chunks of the text. All they end up with is a mini-textbook.

Thus twenty, thirty or more pages of text may boil down to a couple of pages of skeleton outline or spray diagrams. If you were merely looking for extra information to add to what you already know, then your notes from those thirty or so pages may amount to no more than a few lines (or nothing at all).

Making notes in lectures

That last piece of advice also applies to making notes in lectures. One definition of a lecture is: 'A method for conveying the contents of the lecturer's notebook into that of the student without passing through the minds of either party.' Snide, but often true. Some lecturers do seem to content themselves with reading from their notes, or writing them on the board for you to copy. And some students seem satisfied to record as much as possible without pausing to ponder what it's all about.

Making useful notes in lectures depends on understanding what the lecturer means. This, in turn, depends on how you approach the lecture – surveying, questioning and listening – as we discuss in Chapter 7. This listening is a very complex task. Not only must you pick out the lecturer's *main ideas* as he or she speaks, and grasp the overall *structure* of the lecture but also – and *at the same time* – you must decide what is worth noting and what is not.

This is no easy task. Some students deal with it by taking copious notes – often in summary form – and hoping to see some sort of pattern emerge from them after the lecture is over. Others concentrate on following the lecturer's line of argument, taking very few notes even if this means they don't record all the details.

Do you usually make more notes in lectures than your fellow-students do or less? Why do you think this is?

Possibly your practice will vary from one lecturer (or even lecture) to another. You might find it worthwhile thinking about why you write the kind of lecture notes you do.

On the whole, it is probably better to err on the side of too *few* notes rather than too many, *provided*:

1 this better enables you to concentrate on what the lecturer is saying and grasp the meaning and significance of what is said.

2 you are prepared to write up a full set of notes once the lecture is over.

That last point is essential, however full your lecture notes are. By comparison with reading notes they are likely to be scrappy and disorganized. Go away and rethink them.

Recalling a lecture

As soon as possible after the lecture, try to reconstruct it in your mind (like the 'recall' stage of SQ3R which we discuss in Chapter 5). Perhaps the most useful way to recall the lecture is in company with one or two other students – perhaps members of your self-help group (see Chapter 4). Comparing notes, you may find that different people have picked up different points and that, together, you can make a better set of notes – and better sense of what was said – than any one of you did separately.

What form of notes?

Obviously, the form of notes you use will be much influenced by how clearly your lecturer indicates his or her structure. If the structure is clear, then you may be able to work up a reasonable skeleton outline – with headings, sub-headings, numbering, indentation and so on.

Otherwise, you may find it more practical to jot down points as they come, and sort them into a skeleton outline *after* the lecture. This may mean completely rewriting your notes – unless you leave a very wide margin in which to insert headings and numbers alongside your notes.

But, if the lecture content is at all worthwhile, such rewriting (and rethinking) will be a useful exercise in recall.

You may also consider noting the lecture in the form of a spray diagram – so long as you don't let the mechanics involved distract you from thinking about what the lecturer is saying. And, again, you will probably need to tidy it up (perhaps even produce a skeleton outline version) later on when you think back over the lecture.

Notes in discussion groups

It's difficult to say anything very specific about notes in discussion groups – except to be prepared to make some. As we discuss in Chapter 7, such groups vary enormously. At one extreme, discussion may follow after what is virtually a mini-lecture – but with a student delivering it instead of a tutor. At the other extreme, you may have a wide open discussion in which every member is liable to say as much as any other on the topic of the session.

Such an open discussion may also take place, over a period of days or weeks, in computer conferencing (see Chapter 8). But there a complete record of what people said (or rather wrote) remains available for you to browse through after it is over.

You can treat a fellow-student's presentation much as you might a tutor's lecture. In a more free and easy discussion, you need to be very flexible in your note-making. Perhaps all you'll be able to do is jot down a few of the most significant points that emerge. If members of the group make summaries on a board, screen or flipchart, then you may want to include these in your personal notes.

Noting your own ideas

As we mentioned earlier, not all your notes need arise in response to other people's ideas. Many students find the best way of sorting out their own ideas is to sit down with pencil and paper and jot down a few notes.

So, let's say you are sitting and thinking about a particular topic. It could be one you have studied, and you are simply trying to bring back to mind the main issues. It could be a new topic you are about to begin studying seriously and you are wondering what questions you already have about it. It could be a matter of how to tackle an assignment on a topic you are already familiar with.

In all these cases, and others like them, you don't have to go off in search of new information. All you need is in your head. But how do you get it onto paper? (Or onto your computer screen if that's the way you prefer to work.)

Take the case of preparing for an essay. Would you write notes before starting to draft the essay? If so, how would you produce them – and would they take any of the forms we've discussed so far?

Most students jot down some sort of notes before starting to write an essay. But they differ greatly in how they set about it and what sort of notes they feel they need before starting. Perhaps this is something on which you might want to compare experiences with fellow-students?

Brainstorming

One useful approach is 'brainstorming' – just muse upon the topic and jot down *anything* that comes to mind in connection with it. The essence of this approach is to write down everything just as it comes. Ideally, you shouldn't stop to decide whether some items look more useful than others or in what order they might be dealt with. Only when you have run out of ideas, and perhaps have a lengthy list, should you start to consider which look most promising, and how they might be developed and structured into a logical sequence.

Thus, before I began writing this chapter, I jotted down a list of items beginning:

— Why make notes?
— How used?
— Are they used?
— What forms?
— When written?

An ideas map

I then found it helpful to rough out a diagram trying to link up the main ideas I picked out from my list (Figure 6). As you see, it looks rather like a spray diagram, but is much looser. (We might call it an 'ideas map'.) I've

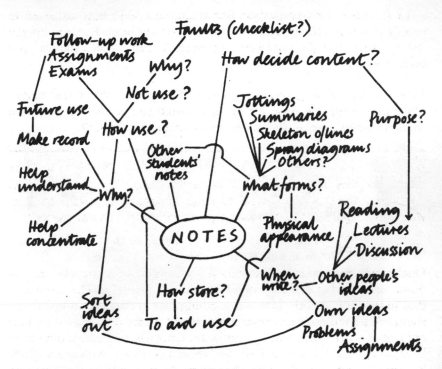

Figure 6: Ideas map

simply jotted down my ideas and drawn lines between those I think have
some sort of connection. It looks a bit of a mess, but it *served its purpose*.
It helped me decide how to structure the chapter and from it I produced
a skeleton outline to guide my first draft.

Sometimes I find it helpful to sketch out an ideas map as *part of* my initial brainstorm rather than after I've finished it. Roughing out such an
'ideas map' may strike you as a useful way of sorting through your ideas
on a topic – regardless of whether you are preparing for an assignment,
and regardless of whether you have first done a brainstorm.

As always, it is up to you to experiment with a variety of approaches
and find out what suits you best. In writing an essay, for example, some
students might be quite confident about launching in with an ideas map
(or even just a list of points) while others (and I'd be one of them) would
not be comfortable unless they had some sort of skeleton outline. And

again, while some will be happy with pencil and paper, others will want to do their mapping or outlining with the help of a computer.

The physical appearance of your notes

The notes we've just been discussing for brainstorming are for instant use. Once they've served their purpose in helping you sort your ideas out you'll probably (though not necessarily) throw them in the waste-basket.

But what if you are writing notes that you expect to use again in the future? Then you need to consider their physical appearance on the page. The grotty appearance of many students' notes, perhaps to the point of illegibility, may be one reason why they make less use of them later than they had originally expected.

Here are some questions to consider in relation to the layout and presentation of your own notes. Tick those you feel you can give a satisfactory answer to.

1 Do I always label my notes so as to show what they are about, where I got them from, and when I made them? ☐

2 If they are in my handwriting, can I still read it? ☐

3 Have I worked out a set of abbreviations that I can use consistently *and* understand when I read them later! ☐

4 Do I leave plenty of white space in and around my writing? (Narrow margins and tightly packed lines of writing squeezed together make pages of notes difficult to read, difficult to add to and difficult to remember – because one page looks much like another.) ☐

5 Do I, for example, break up my material into digestible chunks by using, where possible:

- lists (like this one)? ☐
- indentation (as here)? ☐
- numbered or lettered points? ☐
- headings and sub-headings? ☐
- boxes around important items? ☐

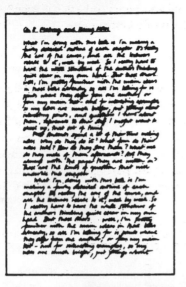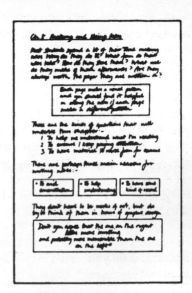

Figure 7: Visual patterns

6 Do I indicate the relative importance of various items by (if I'm writing by hand):

- varying the size of my writing? ☐
- sometimes using CAPITALS? ☐
- underlining words and phrases? ☐
- using different coloured pens (with discretion)? ☐

or (if I'm using a word processor) by using:

- different type styles ☐
- different type sizes ☐
- italics, bold, etc. ☐

7 Do I use drawings or diagrams to capture ideas that cannot be so easily expressed in words and/or to make the page of notes more visually memorable? ☐

If you left many boxes unticked, then you may need to look for ways of improving the legibility, layout and visual clarity of your notes. They don't have to be works of art, but do try to think of them in terms of graphic design. Each page makes a visual pattern *and you should find it helpful when using the notes if each page presents a different pattern. Whatever the subject of the two pages of notes shown in Figure 7, don't you agree that the one on the right looks more inviting, and probably more memorable, than the one on the left?*

Storing and using notes

If you intend to use your notes again sometime after you've written them, then you'll need to decide on a suitable storage system – so that you can find them quickly and easily whenever you want them.

Storing your notes

There are many ways of storing notes. Ideally, you should be able to store all your notes on a given topic *together* – whether you got them from reading or lectures, lab work or field trips, and whether you made them this week or last year. This is more easily done with *ring binders* than with bound notebooks. With a ring binder you have a loose-leaf system. You can open up its steel clips to insert pre-punched sheets of paper and to remove sheets, rewrite them and reorder them as you wish. You can also insert new material – including essays, problems sheets, handouts and stuff you've photocopied as well as notes – wherever you like.

Many students who use computers are storing their notes in directories or files on disk. This can be very effective in some ways, e.g. for hunting down all your mentions of a key term. But inserting material you haven't typed yourself (e.g. photocopies) is not easy; so you may not be able to store all your stuff on one topic in the same place.

Using your notes

One of the running themes of this chapter has been whether and for what purpose you might wish to refer to your notes again at some time after you have written them. Here now is a reminder of some ways you might want to use them. Please tick those you think would be appropriate in your studying.

- Rewriting lecture notes soon afterwards in order to improve my understanding of the lecture ☐

- Comparing notes with fellow-students to see how similarly/differently we have reacted to the same book, lecture or other shared learning experience ☐

- Reading my notes to see which references need following up or what practical work needs doing ☐

- Rewriting old notes to incorporate newer ideas, references to related topics, new reading, etc. ☐

- Referring to earlier notes as an aid in preparing an assignment ☐

- Checking back on ideas I might be hoping to use in my job (or elsewhere in 'real life') ☐

- Trying to refresh my memory about the course ☐

- Reducing notes (i.e. writing one page of 'essentials' from several pages of original notes) perhaps as part of revising for exams ☐

- Other ways of revising for exams ☐

The only way to judge *your* notes is by how well they serve your purpose. They don't have to look like anyone else's.

Follow-up activities

1 Find out how other students make notes.

2 Pair up with a colleague, read the same book and/or attend the same lecture together, compare your notes and discuss why they differ.

3 Try having one of you write notes during a lecture while the other concentrates on following the lecture, then compare your understanding and produce joint notes after the lecture.

4 Experiment with different forms of note-making until you find one (or a combination) that suits you best.

5 Make any amendment to your note-making suggested by your answers to the questions on pages 172–173.

6 If you have a self-help group (see Chapter 4), see if you can get the group to:

● write notes about a shared experience, e.g. a radio talk

● compare notes and try to understand why each person has included this or left out that, or structured them in such-and-such a way

● discuss how each person intends to use the notes in future

● check and discuss each other's notes from time to time, preferably using a checklist of criteria compiled by the group

10
Writing essays and assignments

'I'd never had less than an A or a B, but here I was with a C on this essay. So, I went up to see him and asked why . . . and he said: "Well, you shouldn't have given me all this stuff about Western countries' shortcomings compared with Russia – I've lived there and, believe me, you don't know what it's like. What I meant by evaluating the Soviet system was for you to concentrate on its own internal problems." And I just thought, "Well, why didn't you say that in your essay title, then!" But I'll make sure I suss out what his essays are really after next time, though, won't I?'

As that student's experience reminds us, writing essays is a peculiar business. What could be more odd than explaining something to a person who is supposed to know far more about it than you do? How do you know which points to spell out and which you can assume your reader will take for granted? The task becomes even more tricky if you suspect that your reader has some ideal answer in his or her head that the essay title does not quite reveal!

The value of writing essays

For most students, preparing essays, reports or other written assignments takes up much of their time. The work involved in writing an essay can help them in a variety of ways.

Which two or three of the following would you say are the *chief* benefits that *you* get from the writing of assignments?

1 It encourages me to explore a topic more deeply and purposefully than I might otherwise do ☐

2 It helps me organize my thinking on that topic in order to come up with my own point of view or 'angle' ☐

3 It gives me practice in written communication that will be valuable in areas other than essay writing ☐

4 It gives me an opportunity to find out how well I am coping with the demands of the course ☐

5 It enables my tutor to tell me about my strengths and weaknesses, and how I might improve ☐

6 It enables me to notch up some points towards my final assessment score (or at least impress the people who will probably be marking the final exams) ☐

7 It makes sure I've got useful overviews to revise from in the run-up to exams ☐

8 It gives me practice that will be useful in the exams (since I'll need to write many essays then) ☐

All the above benefits no doubt seem significant to most students at one time or another. Benefits (1) and (2) are perhaps those that would be appreciated by the student with an intrinsic *(and probably* academic *or* personal*) interest in the subject matter. They go with a 'deep-level' approach to one's subject (see Chapter 2). Benefit (3) might appeal to students with an* intrinsic, vocational *bent. Benefits (4) and (5) are important if you are at all uncertain about your progress, or are keen to do better. Benefit (6) sounds fairly cynical, but is sometimes the only one that can realistically be obtained from the kind of essays that get set and the way they are marked in some college departments. Benefits (7) and (8) are very practical considerations when it comes to facing up to the formal examination requirements of a course.*

For all students, though, preparing essays should be seen as *part* of the learning process – not as a troublesome chore that follows it. After we've read, heard and talked about a topic, our minds are awash with ideas, impressions and chunks of information. But we never really get to grips with this experience until we try to write down our own version of it. Making notes is of some help, of course. But there is nothing like the writing of an essay to make us question our ideas, weigh up our impressions, sort out what information is relevant and what is not – and, above all, come up with a reasoned viewpoint on the topic that we can feel is *our own*.

Writing is the crucial step without which learning is incomplete. (Except, of course, for students in areas like acting or catering or interpersonal skills, where 'live performance' plays a similar role in enabling them to *express* their understanding.) Also, since practically every occupation students are likely to enter will demand a similar ability to report in writing – see benefit (3) above – it is clearly a 'life skill'.

So what's the problem?

Different students mention different problems in tackling essays and other written assignments. Which of the following present the most frequent problems for you?

- Understanding what my tutors want from me ☐
- Deciding what I want to get out of doing an assignment ☐
- Squaring what I want with what my tutors want ☐
- Deciding where to look for likely 'raw material' ☐
- Sorting out what is most relevant to the topic ☐
- Deciding on an overall approach or structure ☐
- Getting started on the actual writing ☐
- Keeping to the point ☐
- Good English ☐
- Critiquing and improving my first draft ☐
- Dealing with tutors' comments and criticisms ☐

Clearly, there is no shortage of potential problems. Maybe you've experienced most of them from time to time. However, the rest of this chapter should give you some help in starting to improve on those that give you most trouble.

Let's look at what I see as the seven main stages in dealing with essays and other written assignments.

1 Understanding the context

2 Analysing your task

3 Researching your raw material

4 Planning your essay

5 Writing your essay

6 Critiquing your essay

7 Learning from tutor feedback

Understanding the context

Realistic students, the 'cue-conscious' ones, are likely to examine the nature and role of assignments rather closely. And their approach will be affected by how they size up each assignment within the overall context.

For example, here is the first of some fairly basic questions you should be able to tick off your answers to.

What kinds of written assignment am I going to be asked for on this course, e.g.

- study journal or log-book? ☐
- reports on practical work or field-trips? ☐
- papers for discussion at seminars, etc.? ☐
- reviews of books, articles, etc.? ☐
- notes on problems? ☐
- short essays (say, 1500–2500 words)? ☐
- long essays (say, 2500–4000 words)? ☐
- project reports (4000 words plus)? ☐

If you were uncertain about any of the above items (either for the course you are taking now or one you plan to take soon), maybe you'll want to do some finding out.

Now look at another set of questions. First, tick those you know the answers to. Then put a *ring* round the box if you reckon that knowing the answer can influence the way you *tackle* your assignments.

- How many assignments are set? ☐

- Will the assignments cover all the areas likely to be tested in any final examinations? ☐

- What is the timetable for submitting them? ☐

- To whom must they be submitted? ☐

- Are all the assignments compulsory? ☐

- How soon do I get details of each assignment? ☐

- Do I get any choice of topic within an assignment? ☐

- Will assignments contribute to my final grade or assessment on the course? ☐

- If so, what percentage of the final grade might they account for? ☐

- What penalties might I incur if I don't submit certain assignments? ☐

- Who will be marking the assignments? ☐

- What will the markers be looking for? ☐

- Do the markers have any known preferences (either in subject content or treatment) that I might need to take account off? ☐

- Are there any special requirements of presentation (e.g. layout or references) that I need to follow? ☐

There are many ways in which knowing the answers to questions like these may influence you in tackling essays and other assignments. Look at the first two questions, for example, and read what one student told me:

> *'We soon figured out that the number of assignments we get set during the year doesn't anything like approach the number of topics that are likely to come up in the final exam. But there are several options – different topics you can tackle – within each assignment. So a few of us got together and what we do is we decide which of us is going to write about which of the different topics. Then when we get the essays back with the tutor's marks and comments, we photocopy them, and everybody gets a copy of all the essays. That way, when we start revising for the exam, we've each got commented-on essays covering a far wider range of topics than we've been able to study personally.'*

Clearly, the success of that strategy depends on the quality of the essays and the helpfulness of the tutor's comments. But it is a good example of how knowledge of the total context can affect your assignment strategy. (It is also a good example of the benefits of collaborating with fellow-students.)

Learning the discourse

For many students new to college level work, the last three questions above are the key to success. How do your tutors expect you to write (or talk) about the subject? When you begin studying a new subject you are, in effect, joining a new social group – the group of people who are already expert in that subject. As with any social group (e.g. a street gang, a political party or a religious sect) members have their own distinctive ways of looking at the world, their own specialist jargon and their own accepted ways of expressing ideas and making out a case. These may be quite different from the way we do such things in everyday life (or even in other specialist subjects).

So, learning and practising the ways of the group – or as it is often called, in academic circles, 'the discourse' – is one of the most important things you will be doing in your written work. For many students, learning to write (and thereby think) like a psychologist or a chemical engineer or a geographer can take quite a while – especially if they haven't noticed that there *is* a required form of discourse. Unfortunately, many tutors give you no explicit guidance about the nature of the discourse. You often have to figure it out for yourself from the way the experts think, write and talk and from paying close attention to your tutors' comments about what *you* write. And sometimes you'll need to give up some of your earlier 'common sense' ideas to make way for it (see page 22).

Analysing your task

'Understanding the context' was to do with thinking about your strategy for approaching assignments in general. Now we must focus on tackling an individual assignment task. Many students come to grief because they do not give the matter enough thought – either about what the particular assignment might be demanding from them or about what they might hope to get from doing the assignment.

How much freedom?

Here are some questions to ask in analysing your assessment task and beginning to think about how you might tackle it:

(a) Does this assignment give me a choice from several topics?

(b) If so, how shall I decide which topic to tackle?

- one that I am already familiar with and can write effortlessly about?

- one that sounds pretty tedious, though straightforward, and almost certain to come up in the exam?

- one that sounds interesting but which will involve me in new learning and a more challenging writing task?

(c) Whether I am given a specific topic or get some choice, how *free* am I to approach it as I wish?

Consider question (c) for a moment, and imagine you are a student of politics. Which of the following essay titles might you prefer to tackle and *why*?

(i) 'The political system of any modern Western European state.' ☐

(ii) 'The political system of modern Sweden.' ☐

(iii) 'Comment on the political stability of modern Sweden.' ☐

(iv) 'Explain the political stability of modern Sweden.' ☐

(v) 'Identify and discuss three factors that might help explain the political stability of modern Sweden.' ☐

(vi) 'Identify and evaluate three factors that might help explain the emergence of a stable political system in Sweden despite the massive social and economic changes brought about by the processes of modernization.' ☐

I wonder which one you chose and why. You will notice that the titles become increasingly specific as you go down the list. They therefore leave you less and less freedom to approach the assignment task as you wish.

Students who are 'Syllfs' (see Chapter 2) may prefer titles (i) or (ii). The second apparently gives them free rein to focus on whatever aspects they wish about the political system of Sweden, while the first widens this choice to any Western European country. 'Syllbs', however, may be happier with titles nearer the bottom of the list. The final title, for example, is very explicit about how to tackle the assignment.

Factors in choosing

Of course, the above titles would not be offered as alternatives. You'd see just one of them, perhaps among a group of quite different options. You might be hesitant about choosing such a title as (ii) or (iii) because of a suspicion that the markers might be looking for something specific (but undisclosed) in your answers. For instance, (ii) gives no indication that 'stability' is a feature of the political system they'd particularly wish you to comment on. And (iii) gives no clue as to how many factors they think important or why the 'stability' needs accounting for anyway. Might you miss some unstated expectation by going for too wide open a topic, however challenging it might be? (This is what seems to have happened to the student quoted at the beginning of this chapter.)

So, just some of the factors in deciding which assignment task to tackle might be:

● how much choice you get

● how interested you are in the various topics offered

- how much you already know about the topics

- how much you feel you could usefully learn by tackling a newish topic

- how much time you have available

- which topics you know will be marked by tutors who give useful comments and criticisms of students' work

- how confident you can be that your approach to a particular topic will not be miles away from what the marker will accept

Perhaps you can think of yet other factors that influence you in *your* particular situation.

The last factor listed above is important for all students except those who are so intrinsically motivated that they don't care whether they get their tutors' approval or not. Few are in this happy position. Unfortunately, many tutors aren't too clear what exactly they are looking for when they set assignments. (The first two topics in the list above may well have been set by such tutors.) But they'll pounce on you fast enough if you don't tackle it in a way they recognize as worthwhile – i.e. if you haven't got the hang of the 'discourse'.

What is expected?

However, some tutors do give you a clue as to how they want you to approach the topic. This you can detect from key verbs like 'compare', 'review', 'analyse' and so on that they've used in the assignment title.

Underline any key verbs of this type you can see in the six essay titles about Swedish politics mentioned above.

The key verbs mentioned in the six titles are 'comment on' (iii), 'explain' (iv), 'identify and discuss' (v) and 'identify and evaluate' (vi). Titles (i) and (ii) offer no such clues.

If you haven't already had occasion to do so, it is *vital* that you ponder the differences between such verbs. Students lose countless marks on essays – especially in examinations where it matters most – by, say, merely describing when they were asked to 'compare', or defining when they were asked to 'analyse'. Admittedly, a vague verb like 'comment on' or 'discuss' does leave it rather open as to how probing you are expected to be. But it is usually safer, in such cases, to be more probing rather than less so.

There is a *glossary* of such key terms at the end of this chapter. You may find it helpful in deciding just what your tutors are expecting from you. Look now at how I've defined the terms, and try to list in your notebook three terms, say, that sound *least* like what your tutors will normally expect from you and three that sound *most* like what they expect.

It depends what sort of course you are doing, but if you are studying in higher education, I would expect your list of 'least like' terms to contain words like 'define', 'describe', 'illustrate', 'list' and 'state'. In your other list I would expect to see terms like 'analyse', 'assess', 'discuss', 'to what extent', and 'justify'.

In short, I imagine you will usually be faced with writing the kind of assignment that demands from you some kind of *critical argument* – not just a compilation of relevant facts. (If I'm wrong about this, don't worry. What I have to say from here on applies just as well to all sorts of assignments.)

Perhaps your tutors haven't used very explicit verbs in their assignment titles. Perhaps they haven't used any at all – as in (i) and (ii) in the politics titles we looked at earlier.

If they haven't given you any guidance as to what they expect, go and ask them (perhaps with equally concerned colleagues) what sort of approach they are looking for. If they say, 'That's up to you,' then they'll hardly be able to claim later that you've taken a wrong one.

Researching your raw material

Once you have decided on your title you'll need to research into its subject matter. Normally you will need to go to a variety of sources for the material out of which you will shape your essay.

Sources of ideas

Which of the following sources might you usefully consult for the types of assignment you'll be writing?

- None but my own experience and thinking ability ☐
- Books and journals required for my course ☐
- New materials suggested by my tutor for the task ☐
- Other materials mentioned in the suggested reading that I think worth following up ☐
- Primary sources, e.g. fossils or historical documents ☐
- Reference books and encyclopedias ☐
- Internet (World Wide Web) resources ☐
- Computer discussion groups ☐
- Laboratory or workshop experience ☐
- Fieldwork or other experience away from college ☐
- Discussions with people who have relevant knowledge ☐

The type and variety of sources you consult will no doubt depend on the nature of your subject and the scale of the assignment you are tackling. Don't overlook informal sources of ideas. While the assignment is simmering in your mind, keep alert for useful thoughts that crop up unexpectedly – in lectures, seminars and tutorials, in your own personal experience or leisure reading and/or television viewing, and in casual conversation with fellow-students or with tutors.

Three practical points

Keep a notebook

It's wise to carry about with you a little notebook, with a page or so devoted to each assignment or project you are working towards. Then, if ideas crop up or you come across a useful quotation or example, you can jot it down on paper before it fades from the memory. Many successful students (and authors) claim they owe much of their success to always having such a notebook with them. They never let a good idea escape unrecorded.

Start researching early

Begin thinking about how you'll tackle your assignment as soon as you know the title. Even if your tutor gives you a month or more, don't wait until the week before the deadline before you give the matter any thought. There are two good reasons for making an early start:

a) In classes or in casual conversation, and especially in your general reading, you may quite accidentally come across ideas that would be relevant to your assignment. But if you have not already given some thought to your assignment topic, you may fail to appreciate their significance.

b) We all know how we get some of our most brilliant ideas when we are thinking about something entirely different – or about nothing at all. Somehow the unconscious mind goes on chewing away at our problems even when our attention is otherwise engaged. So leave as much time as possible between first thinking about your assignment and the day when you must sit down to write it. Give your unconscious mind a fair chance to help sort it out for you.

Record your sources

Whatever the source of your ideas, do make a note of where you get them from. In writing down anyone else's idea that you think may have a bearing on your assignment, record the title of the book or article (and who published it, when and where), or the name of the speaker from whom you heard it.

You *must* give credit to these sources if you use them in your assignment. It creates a very bad impression with your tutor if, through carelessness or lapse of memory, you present her or him with ideas as if they were your own but which he or she recognizes as coming from other authors. This is equally important with Internet resources.

Avoid plagiarism

Worse still if you use, without acknowledgement, not just other people's ideas but also their very words. This ugly practice goes by the equally ugly name of *plagiarism*. It is becoming something of a problem with Internet resources where students can so easily 'copy and paste' material straight from World Wide Web pages into their word-processed essays.

Researching questioningly

For most students, the bulk of their researching will be done through reading. But don't just start bashing through an armful of books or surfing the Internet in the vague hope that something useful will pop out. To get results, you must read actively and purposefully. And one of the best ways to ensure this is to look for answers to some specific *questions*.

The place to start is with your assignment title, which may itself be a question. But this will be too broad. You'll need to break it down by asking yourself questions about it. These questions can then guide you in your reading. One way into asking questions is to remember Rudyard Kipling's famous verse – a comment on his experience as a journalist:

> 'I had six serving men and true
> They taught me all I knew
> Their names were *What* and *Why* and *When*
> And *How* and *Where* and *Who*.'

But mostly you'll find that assignment titles, however brief, will spark off their own questions quite easily – so long as you look at them questioningly.

For instance, suppose you were asked to prepare an essay on: 'Current research into how students learn.'

Try to write at least three questions you might ask yourself to help start your investigations into that topic.

There is no end to the questions you might have asked yourself. Here are just a few that occur to me, and yours will probably be quite different:

- Who is doing the research?
- What are the key publications?
- Which aspects of student learning are being looked at?
- What forms does the research take?
- Are there any special difficulties or problems attached to it?
- Have any new findings emerged about how students learn?
- Have any approaches to learning proved better than others?
- Could students benefit by knowing of the research findings?
- Could tutors benefit by knowing of them?
- How do I feel about students being researched in such ways?

Always try to think out *and write down* a few questions in this way before you begin your research for an essay. As you read, and talk with people, you will come up with further questions, usually more specific ones. And perhaps some of those on your original list will seem less relevant. But almost any set of initial questions are better than none in giving you some direction as you begin to come to grips with the subject matter of your assignment.

You may also think it helpful to build some sense of urgency into your research by giving yourself a *deadline* by which to finish it. This you can do by scheduling yourself a day by which you expect to be prepared enough to sit down and write your essay.

By that time, you should have done all the research you need, except perhaps for the odd fact or reference that may need to be verified. You should have all the information you need for the essay. And, after all the questioning and thinking (conscious and unconscious) you've done, you should have more than a glimmering of the approach you'll be taking, the angle you'll want to give your assignment or the argument you'll want to pursue.

Planning your essay

Think twice before you jump straight from research into writing the first sentence of your essay. I know that many students start with the first word and soldier on until they reach the last, and then stop! All too often, however, such attempts start off in a flurry of enthusiasm only to fizzle out a few paragraphs later for want of a sense of direction.

There is no harm in jotting down a few possible sentences for your essay. This you may have been doing as they occurred to you at any time since you first started thinking about it. But it may be unwise to launch into writing your essay until you have some kind of outline or *plan*.

Your purpose

To begin with, remind yourself of your purpose in writing the essay. What sort of essay is it going to be? What do you want to get across in it? What is your tutor expecting from you? Think about the title again – and examine the key verbs (if there are any).

If it is just a title (like the one I mentioned about research into how students learn), you need to decide, for example:

- Must I cover the whole topic or can I concentrate on one aspect (e.g. how *science* students learn or how students in general tackle *reading*)?

- To what extent am I expected merely to *describe* the research and to what extent must I attempt to *evaluate* it or make proposals as to how it might be applied?

If your title takes the form of a question, you need to decide what might be an appropriate form of answer.

For example, suppose your title asked: 'Would you be in favour of weekly sessions on study skills for students in their first year of college?' Which of these forms of answer do you think might be most appropriate?

A A straightforward *yes* or *no* (or *'I'm not sure'*)

B A definite *yes* or *no*, backed up by my own experiences

C An analysis of some alternative forms such study sessions might take, based on the findings that have emerged from research into how students learn

D Much the same as C but ending up with a definite statement as to whether I am *for* or *against*

E Like C but weighing up the pros and cons of different ways of running such sessions and indicating which kinds I might recommend and which not

---

Its use of the word 'favour' suggests that the question expects some kind of evaluation. But it's not asking just for a blunt opinion, as someone might in a bar-room conversation. So answer A is clearly not enough; and even B sounds like it might be just a gut reaction with a few personal anecdotes thrown in by way of justification.

A college-level essay – whatever the precise form of discourse – will be asking for something more considered and analytical. Your tutors are probably interested not so much in your eventual conclusion – and you may very properly end up undecided, anyway – as in *how you set about examining the issues involved.* What evidence do you see as being relevant to the question? How do you evaluate it? What relationships do you see within it? What might be the implications?

So answer C looks better – at least there's some intention of looking into the evidence from research and using it to analyse the kinds of study-skills session that might be held. But there is no mention of any attempt to evaluate the various possibilities. Answer D does add the evaluative element, but seems perhaps rather too determined to come up with a definitive, overall *yes/no* conclusion. Perhaps answer E is safer in recognizing that research findings may support certain kinds of study-skills session rather more than others.

So, in addition to the two mentioned earlier, three more questions to ask yourself before planning your essay might be:

- Are my tutors looking for a reasoned *argument* (rather than merely my personal opinion and/or a catalogue of facts)?

- How many *different* (but arguable) viewpoints might different people have on the issue involved?

- What is *my* viewpoint? How can I best get it across?

No doubt other such questions will occur to you that relate more directly to the sort of essay you normally have to plan. Write one down in your notebook, just as an example.

One student replied to that last invitation by saying: 'How can I make sure my essay has an acceptable amount of Marxist/feminist/monetarist slant to it?'

Select from your material

An essential part of planning is to weigh up, and select from, the material you have collected in your research. You may have pages of notes. Which of them are relevant? Which are not?

Usually you will find that not all the material you have gathered is useable. Some of the factual material you have collected will seem unrelated to whatever themes you now realize you want to pursue. Some of the ideas you picked up, even if relevant to your themes, may now seem flimsy and unsupported by sufficient evidence. Such material will need discarding. There's more than enough of this sort of padding and makeweight in student essays already.

At the same time, ensure you have enough material (e.g. specific examples and relevant quotations or results) to back up whatever themes or viewpoints or arguments you will be putting forward. Such material is not padding. Indeed it is vital to the credibility and strength of your argument.

Write an outline

For most students, working out some sort of structure or outline seems a necessary preliminary to writing an essay. Not all take the same approach, however. Which of the approaches mentioned by these four students seems best for you?

A *'I don't do any sort of outline; I just start writing, not even where I know the final essay will begin – and after I've written a few paragraphs some sort of plan begins to become clear to me and I often tear up what I've written and start again quite differently. I usually don't know what I'm after until I see what I've written.'* ☐

B *'I start by deciding roughly how many paragraphs I've got space for, what point I want to make in each paragraph and where I need to bring in different bits of evidence and that – it's hard sometimes because one thing often merges into another – but really I'm not happy to start writing until I've got an outline that would tell the tutor almost as much as the essay I write from it.'* ☐

C *'All I need is my final paragraph. I write that out first – my conclusions, the essentials of the way I've interpreted the topic, "on the one hand this, on the other hand that, but on balance so-and-so . . ." sort of thing. I spend a fair bit of time on that, several drafts maybe – but once I've got it right, I usually just start at the beginning and bash on towards that final paragraph.'* ☐

D *'I've got to plan myself a basic framework – beginning, middle and end. I decide roughly how many words in each of the three sections, and I'll list the probable sequence of points in the middle section – perhaps only half a side of paper. But I must have this to start with, even if I change it as I go along.'* ☐

These are four very different approaches. For all I know, yours is some-thing else again. My own approach is usually most like that of student D although, like A, I am quite used to finding that what I am writing takes on such a life of its own that I only discover what I was really trying to say once I see what I've already said. I also see some virtue in student C's faith in having a very clear idea as to what you are writ-ing towards – but I'd need more than a perfectly formed final paragraph to set me on my way. Student B's approach I would find least easy to work with. Having written what sounds like such an exquisitely detailed outline, I think I would have no enthusiasm left for turning it into lively prose.

How detailed an outline?

The detail with which you need to plan in advance depends, in part, on how willing you are to write *more than one draft* of your essay. Clearly, this will be easier if you are word processing on a computer than if you are writing by hand (or even with a typewriter). If you are happy to draft and redraft (as student A above probably does), then you may need do little more than jot down a few key words before you start writing. If you intend to write just one, or at most two, drafts, then you'll need to do much more planning in advance.

Here are some advantages of having an outline:

1 It helps you see your essay *as a whole* – helping to ensure that every paragraph contributes towards the total picture.

2 It makes sure you leave out nothing vital and avoid repetition.

3 It allows you, once started, to write fluently without having to chew your pen and lose energy from your writing.

4 If you happen to be writing in an examination and time runs out on you, you may gain more marks from submitting a clear outline than you would from a half-finished essay.

Possibly, you can think of disadvantages also. For instance, some students, having worked out a plan, may become blind to better approaches that suggest themselves once they've started writing. On balance, however, I would recommend you do try producing some kind of outline. For example:

A basic framework

Here is a simple three-point plan that you may have used before. It is useful as a framework for a wide variety of essays and assignments:

1 Introduction
   A Comment on topic of essay. (e.g. What do you understand by it? What are the main issues? And so on.)

   B Which aspects will you be dealing with? Why? What will be your general approach in the essay?

2 The main body
   A List the main points you want to get across. If you reckon on around 100 words per paragraph on average, this may give you an idea of how many paragraphs you'll have to get these points across in.

   B Check that your points follow one another in some kind of logical sequence or reasoned argument.

   C Jot down the examples and illustrations you'll use in presenting these main ideas.

3 Conclusion
   A Sum up your main ideas.

   B Offer a firm or tentative conclusion.

   C Point out any wider implications or future trends or scope for further investigation.

I have suggested in Chapter 5 that one of your tasks in reading is to uncover the framework of the *author's* thinking. When planning your writing, your task is rather the reverse – to set out the framework of your own thinking. You'll probably be able to sketch out a framework on one side of a sheet of paper. (A 'spray diagram', perhaps followed by a 'skeleton outline', as described in Chapter 9, may be useful in this.)

Writing your essay

Finally, you are ready to start writing what, ideally, will be a *first draft* of your essay. Write as well as you can, but be prepared to make changes later. Don't feel you must write the paragraphs in the order in which they will be read. If you find the beginning difficult, start somewhere else – even with a draft of the final paragraph if that suits you. Anyway, get something written as soon as possible, even in the knowledge that you may well scrap it later. Try to bash out your first rough draft in one sitting if at all possible.

Here are the four basic points to bear in mind:

● Know what you want to say

● Remember why you want to say it

● Keep in mind the person to whom you are saying it

● Say it as simply and directly as you can

I've already said enough about the first three. Let's concentrate on the fourth:

Writing simply and directly

The best one-sentence guide to effective writing I've ever heard is: 'Write like you talk.' In my own writing (e.g. as in this book), I try to put down on paper what I would say to my reader if he or she were sitting there in front of me. In other words, I aim for a style that is informal and fairly conversational – but without being matey or chatty. Whether such an approach would be acceptable to your tutors is something I leave you to decide.

Writing simply

Under this heading, I'll suggest using the most simple (and therefore direct) words, sentences and paragraphs:

Use simple words
(a) Don't refer to 'the author' (meaning yourself) or 'the reader' if you can reasonably say 'I' or 'you' ☐

(b) Don't use several words where one will do – e.g. not 'in the great majority of cases' but 'usually' ☐

(c) Use everyday words – e.g. not 'relinquish', 'terminate' and 'exacerbate' but 'give up', 'end' and 'worsen' ☐

(d) Avoid long-winded phrases and pompous-sounding gobbledegook – e.g. not 'They exhibited economy in the deployment of veracity' but 'They lied' ☐

(e) Use precise words rather than general, abstract ones – e.g. not 'Extreme danger is associated with the incorrect operation of this equipment' but 'Unless you keep the safety shield down, this machine may kill you' ☐

(f) Use active verbs – e.g. not 'An experiment was carried out' but 'We carried out an experiment' ☐

Tick each suggestion you think would be approved by your tutors.

If you suspect your tutors might disapprove of some of these, it might be worth showing them the list. If your subject is science-based, for example, you may find some tutors object to items (a) and (f).

Simplify your sentences

Consider the following suggestions:

● Keep your sentences short (rarely more than twenty words). ☐

Short sentences will:

 ● help you avoid grammatical errors

 ● help you spot them more easily if you do make them

 ● save you from many punctuation problems

● *Avoid* writing, wherever possible, sentences which, like this one, having phrases and clauses sprouting within them – each with their own qualifications (some more, and some less, to the point than others) to make – are not only too long but also too complex for easy reading, and are usually better split into several shorter ones. ☐

Keep your paragraphs simple

● Start each paragraph with your 'topic sentence' which carries the main idea; *or* ☐

● Lead up to the main idea as a later (perhaps the final) sentence ☐

● Use the rest of the paragraph to elaborate on the main idea or else lead up to it ☐

● If you've written a paragraph in which you believe the main idea is implied by the whole paragraph and not stated explicitly in any one sentence, make sure you haven't just been waffling or rambling ☐

● If one of your paragraphs contains more than one main idea, make each idea instead the topic of a separate paragraph ☐

Tick any of the above suggestions you think might be worth paying more attention to in your assignments.

Your complexity quotient

How successful are you in writing simply and directly? There are various ways in which you can estimate how straightforward your readers will find your prose. Here is one reasonably quick and reliable way of measuring how simply and directly you are writing:

(a) Select a page of your writing at random

(b) Count how many sentences you have written

(c) Count the number of words with three or more syllables per sentence

(d) Divide (c) by (b) to find the average number of 'long' words per sentence

If this average (call it your Complexity Quotient, or CQ) exceeds three, your writing will be more difficult than that of most novelists.

Try this test on:

1 a page from this book: CQ = . . .

2 a page from one of your standard textbooks: CQ = . . .

3 a page from one of your own essays: CQ = . . .

Does this comparison suggest anything to you?

I can't know what results you've got and we'd be wrong to build too much on comparing just three pages. But I'd guess that this book will have a lower CQ than most textbooks. And I hope that your CQ will not be higher than theirs.

Critiquing your essay

If time allows, put your first draft aside for a couple of days. It is a great mistake to work so close to your deadline that you have no choice but to hand in your first draft. Changes will almost certainly be needed.

Even a day or so's break can give you quite a new perspective on your work. You will come back to it afresh and be able to look at it more objectively. You will be able to assess it *critically* – much as your reader will. If you can get a friend or fellow-student to do this also, so much the better.

Here are some questions you might ask about your work. Check through them and tick off those that sound applicable to the sort of assignments you write.

Purpose
- Am I still clear what my purposes were in writing the assignment? ☐
- Am I satisfied I set about them in an appropriate way? ☐
- To what extent do I feel I have attained them? ☐
- Is my topic clearly stated? ☐
- Have I identified the essential issues? ☐
- Have I made clear my intended approach? ☐

Content
- Is it clear what main ideas I am expressing in each paragraph? ☐
- Are my points properly supported by examples and argument? ☐
- Are my facts correct, complete and up to date? ☐
- Are any quotations I've used really relevant? ☐
- Have I kept an appropriate balance between my own ideas and those of other people? ☐

- Have I made clear which ideas are not my own? ☐
- Have I avoided bias and admitted alternative views? ☐

Structure and style
- Does the assignment have about the expected number of words? ☐
- Will the structure of my essay be clear to the reader? ☐
- Have I used headings where these might help the reader? ☐
- Does each paragraph contain just one main idea? ☐
- Is there a link between one main idea and the next? ☐
- Do my conclusions follow logically from my evidence? ☐
- Have I used graphs, tables or diagrams where appropriate? ☐
- Do my final paragraphs bring the essay to a satisfactory conclusion? ☐
- Are my words and sentences short enough? (Do I have a CQ of three or less? – see above.) ☐
- Have I avoided mistakes in spelling, punctuation and grammar? ☐
- Does the essay read smoothly and easily? (If in doubt, try reading it *aloud*. Anything you find hard to say is likely to prove hard to read as well.) ☐
- Have I followed the expected 'conventions' – e.g. in footnotes, quotations, bibliography, etc.? ☐

I hope the checklist above will form the basis of one you can devise for yourself and use as a matter of course every time you finish the first draft of an assignment.

Be strict in asking yourself the questions you include in your checklist, for your readers will no doubt be asking very similar questions themselves. *Rewrite* your assignment to eliminate whatever weaknesses you have uncovered.

Physical presentation

It is often not enough merely to have good ideas and express them well. Your assignment also needs to look attractive. Research has shown that the *same* essay can be given hugely different marks depending on the quality of the handwriting in which it is presented. So be careful about the physical appearance of your final draft. Make sure it is neat, clearly laid out – with wide margins for your tutor to write comments – and either impeccably written or, where possible, typed or printed out from a word-processor.

By the way, assignments do occasionally go missing after being handed in to a tutor. Photocopying is a very cheap way of insuring against the inconvenience and aggravation such a loss might cause you. Never let any important document out of your hands without keeping a copy of your own.

Learning from tutor feedback

You've researched your topic, you've drafted and redrafted your assignment and you've got it to your tutor. Is it now all over bar the marking? No, ideally you should still be able to *learn* from the comments and criticisms your tutor makes in response to what you've written.

I know that not everyone takes kindly to criticism. But your tutor's criticism and comments may help give you a new perspective on the topic you've just tackled. They may also help you in your approach to *future* assignments.

Tutors' evaluations

Unfortunately, students don't always feel the comments they get are as helpful as they might be. Here are some examples of students' remarks about tutors' comments:

A *'It takes so long to get an essay back that I've sometimes written two or three more by then – so the comments are too late to help me with those essays and I find it too difficult to think my way back into the original essay to make the comments worth thinking about. I just look at the mark, really.'* ☐

B *'His comments are too vague, or else negative – "slipshod argument", "surely not?", "style!", "incoherent". He's just sounding off. It doesn't help me at all.'* ☐

C *'She says quite useful things, but it's all to do with the particular assignment. There's not much to go on for helping with other assignments. And it doesn't tell me much about my progress over the course as a whole.'* ☐

Might any of these comments apply to any of your tutors?

The first two are very common complaints. However thoughtful and well meant the comments, if they arrive weeks after you've forgotten about the essay (student A), they're not as likely to help you learn from the assignment as if they had come when it was still fresh in your mind. And vague or negative comments (student B) are also unhelpful – the vague ones give you no indication as to how you might improve and the negative ones are likely to make you feel so hostile that you pay them little attention even if there is some truth in them. Student C may or may not be right in thinking there is nothing he can learn for future assignments because the comments he gets are too specific to each particular assignment. He certainly feels that the comments are not giving him much of a clue as to how the tutor thinks he is progressing over the course as a whole.

The role of tutor feedback

The fact is, tutors should be able to give you comments and criticisms that help you:

1 Review the present piece of work

2 Prepare for future assignments

3 Assess how well you are mastering the aims of the course – and your subject's form of discourse.

Here, for example, are a few brief tutor comments of the kind that students have said were helpful:

● 'Comment on the results, Chris. Why is there, do you think, such a difference between the least and the greatest? Should these be taken into the average?'

● 'Yes, it is very difficult to assess the effectiveness of the party, either locally or nationally, in this role. In this sort of case, it can be useful to quote an example on a local issue known to you.'

- 'Your answer is OK as far as it goes but you do not show why the drop in IE is so large. Look again at Figure 7 in the text and ask yourself what is so special about the electronic structure of neon and how does it differ from that of sodium.'

- 'Your ability to be analytical about a subject continues to improve. (I particularly liked your distinction between the varieties of prejudice.) But I fear you are still rather too liable to offer unsubstantiated personal opinion as if to clinch an argument. For instance, what evidence would you give for the statement I've underlined in your final paragraph?'

The interesting thing about these comments is that they have the flavour of *dialogue*. The tutors seem to be seeking clarification, evidence or amplification, or they are drawing students' attention to errors or anomalies, but in such a way as to *stretch* their thinking. In fact, helpful commenting probably depends more on them asking you stimulating questions than on telling you what they think you should have written.

Do you feel satisfied with the feedback your tutors give you on your assignments? If not, what would you welcome from them that you are not getting at present? What might you do to get matters improved?

Seeking better feedback

If you feel less than satisfied, bring your concerns to your tutors' attention. Naturally, you will need to do this tactfully, and it might be as well to do it in company with a group of fellow-students who feel as you do. If you are studying on campus, ask the head of your department if you can have a group discussion about how students and tutors see the role of comments and criticisms.

It might help to show your tutors examples of the kind of criticisms you have found helpful in the past. In return, you might ask them to discuss with you the criteria they use in assessing your assignments. They might even be persuaded to let you see some sample essays and show you how they would set about assessing them and commenting on them.

At the very least, try to get your tutors (as a group) to commit themselves to:

(a) giving you comments that are intended to:

    (i) indicate your strengths and weaknesses

    (ii) help you build on your strengths and overcome your weaknesses

(b) getting these to you as soon as possible after you have handed in the assignment

(c) being available to discuss these comments with you if you wish

What if you still end up getting comments that don't help you? Then make an appointment with the tutor concerned, take along your assignment and ask quite frankly whether she or he can suggest a couple of ways in which it might be improved, or ways in which you might approach similar tasks more productively in future.

Your own evaluations

In the end, however, regardless of the help you do or do not get from tutors, you have to make your own evaluation. You'll have evaluated your assignment already, in draft form, before you handed it in. Always try to spare some energy to look at it again, along with whatever comments you can get from your tutor, when it is returned to you.

Ask yourself: 'What have I learned – about this topic, about this subject, about this kind of assignment, about this tutor, about myself – that might be helpful to me in future?' The commitment to evaluating your own experience in this way, and learning something useful from it, is probably one of the most worthwhile habits to be acquired from a college education. It will be of value to you long after the subject matter you have learned has become redundant.

There is always more than one way of looking at any given assignment topic. Make sure you have considered at least two before you start arguing the case from your own viewpoint.

Follow-up activities

1 Estimate the Complexity Quotient of one or two of your essays. Analyse your writing (using the lists on pages 196–198), and consider ways in which it might be improved.

2 Reread one or two of your recent essays and critique them using the checklist on pages 199–200. Compare your reactions with the comments made by your tutor. How helpful do you think your tutor's comments are?

3 Discuss with fellow-students the extent to which they are satisfied with the kind of feedback on assignments they get from tutors. If it is less than satisfactory, what might your group do to encourage tutors to provide more helpful feedback?

4 Get together with some of your colleagues to discuss alternative approaches to a given assignment topic, perhaps using group 'brainstorming' (see Chapter 9).

5 Arrange with one or two fellow-students (perhaps in a self-help group) to critique one another's assignments in draft form. Then compare your assessment of one another's strengths and weaknesses with the tutor's comments when the resulting assignments are returned.

6 Consider the advantages of giving one another photocopies of assignments that have been well received by tutors.

7 Discuss with your colleagues whether tutors might be asked to let your group see copies of some 'specimen answers' (good, bad and acceptable) to help make clear the criteria they use in marking.

8 Consider learning to use a computer for word-processing – to ease your assignment writing (and rewriting).

Glossary of essay terms

What they say	*What they (perhaps) mean*
Account for	Explain, clarify, give the reasons for. (Quite different from 'Give an account of' which is more like 'Describe in detail'.)
Analyse	Break an issue down into its component parts, discuss them and show how they interrelate.

What they say	*What they (perhaps) mean*
Argue	Make a case, based on appropriate evidence and logically structured, for and/or against some given point of view.
Assess	Consider the value or importance of something, paying due attention to positive, negative and disputable aspects, and citing the judgements of any known authorities as well as your own.
Comment on	Too vague to be sure, but safe to assume it means something more than 'describe' or 'summarize' and more likely implies 'analyse' or 'assess'.
Compare	Identify the characteristics or qualities two or more things have in common (but probably pointing out their differences as well).
Contrast	Point out the differences between two things (but probably identifying their similarities as well).
Criticize	Spell out your judgement as to the value or truth of something, indicating the criteria on which you base your judgement and citing specific instances of how the criteria apply in this case.
Define	Make a statement as to the meaning or interpretation of something, giving sufficient detail so as to allow it to be distinguished from similar things.
Describe	Say what a thing looks, tastes, smells, sounds or feels like, or spell out the main aspects of an idea or topic or the sequence in which a series of things happened.
Discuss	Much the same as 'comment on' (see above).
Enumerate	List some relevant items, possibly in continuous prose (rather than note form) – and perhaps 'describe' them (see above) as well.
Evaluate	Like 'assess' (see above).

What they say	*What they (perhaps) mean*
Explain	Tell how things work or how they came to be the way they are, including perhaps some need to 'describe' and to 'analyse' (see above).
To what extent . . .?	Explore the case for a stated proposition or explanation, much in the manner of 'assess' and 'criticize' (see above), probably arguing for a less than total acceptance of the proposition.
How far . . .?	Similar to 'To what extent . . .?' (see above).
Identify	Pick out what you regard as the key features of something, perhaps making clear the criteria you use in doing so.
Illustrate	Similar to 'explain' (see above) but probably asking for the quoting of specific examples or statistics or the drawing of maps, graphs, sketches, etc.
Interpret	Clarify something or 'explain' (see above), perhaps indicating how the thing relates to some other thing or way of looking at things.
Justify	Express valid reasons for accepting a particular interpretation or conclusion, probably including the need to 'argue' (see above) a case.
List	Like 'enumerate' (see above), but possibly even in note form and probably without any need to describe.
Outline	Indicate the main features of a topic or sequence of events, possibly setting them within a clear structure or framework to show how they interrelate.
Prove	Demonstrate the truth of something by offering irrefutable evidence and/or a logical sequence of statements leading from evidence to conclusion.
Reconcile	Show how two apparently opposed or mutually exclusive ideas or propositions can be seen to be similar in important respects, if not identical. Involves need to 'analyse' and 'justify' (see above).

What they say	*What they (perhaps) mean*
Relate	Either 'explain' (see above) how things happened or are connected in a cause-and-effect sense, or may imply 'compare' and 'contrast' (see above).
Review	Survey a topic, with the emphasis on 'assess' rather than 'describe' (see above).
State	Express the main points of an idea or topic, perhaps in the manner of 'describe' or 'enumerate' (see above).
Summarize	'State' (see above) the main features of an argument, omitting all superfluous detail and side-issues.
Trace	Identify the connection between one thing and another either in a developmental sense over a period of time, or else in a cause-and-effect sense. May imply both 'describe' and 'explain' (see above).

NB 1 The above are *not* definitive. If your tutors use the terms in the left-hand column, it is up to you to discover what *they* mean by them!

    2 Furthermore, some of their assignment titles may use no such terms or 'action phrases'. So you will have to use other ways of deciding what they might be expecting from you.

11
Dealing with examinations

'With most courses, if we're enjoying them, we can forget about the fact that there'll be an exam at the end of it. We tell ourselves we'll sort that out when the time comes – it's not what it's all about. But sometimes as you get nearer the end of the course you can't help thinking the exam is exactly what it's all been about – it's the only thing. It's the big unknown. No, it's not a matter of life and death – it's more important than that!'

Clearly, examinations arouse strong feelings, and most readers of this book will have examinations to deal with. Of course, there are some students, especially on vocational training courses, who don't have their learning formally assessed at all. Others have continuous assessment instead of examinations. But, if you are like most students, you will face examinations sooner or later – and they will help determine your future.

How do you feel about exams?

I'll have both downbeat and upbeat things to say about examinations in this chapter. So let's get the downbeat out of the way first. It's good therapy to get one's potential anxieties out into the open as soon as possible – look at them rationally – and then go on to build a positive strategy that will minimize or overcome them.

Which of the following effects might an unsatisfactory exam result have on your future? (And which of those would concern you most?)

- I might be given extra work to do ☐
- I might be required to resit the exam ☐
- I might not be allowed to continue in my course ☐
- I might be required to take a course again ☐
- I might be refused entry into certain other courses ☐
- I might not be allowed to continue in college ☐
- I might not be able to get the level of qualification that I am working for ☐
- I might not be able to qualify at all ☐
- I might not get the kind of career I want ☐
- I might be put off education for good ☐
- I might lose face with people important to me ☐
- I might hate myself for having wasted so much time ☐
- I might feel I'm a failure for some time to come ☐

Obviously, some exams are more critical than others. And different people have more at stake than others. The first of the outcomes I've listed above might not trouble you very much – whereas the last two might have quite a damaging effect on your self-esteem, and make you feel, unjustly, less competent in many other aspects of your life.

It's not surprising, then, that many students view examinations with anxiety. Many feel a bit that way about continuous assessment also, but as one put it:

> *'Comparing continuous assessment with examinations is like comparing months of nagging toothache with the short sharp pain of having a tooth removed.'*

Levels of anxiety

For many people, exams bring out all their underlying fears about being weighed in the balance and found inadequate – or of being totally out of control of their situation.

Which of the following student remarks do you feel is closest to *your* present feelings about important exams?

A *'I wouldn't say I take them in my stride, but I can't honestly say they give me any sleepless nights.'* ☐

B *'No, I won't go bananas. I'll just ration my time out more carefully and think positively.'* ☐

C *'I know I'm under more strain when exams come round, but I just play a lot more squash – that's my way of working off the pressure.'* ☐

D *'I've started smoking again. What more can I say?'* ☐

E *'I get depressed when other students tell me about all the areas they've been looking into and I realize I haven't done anything about them, by how other students seem to have covered so much more of the work than I have and there's no time left to catch up.'* ☐

F *'There's so much to remember – I can't believe my memory's good enough to cope with it all.'* ☐

G *'I can get so paralysed with fear that I couldn't think what to revise or get up the willpower to do it even if someone told me.'* ☐

H *'I'm that panicky and depressed I feel like going off and never coming back.'* ☐

I *'Of course I'm worried and anxious. Who wouldn't be? But I need it. It's the only way I can work up enough steam to get the work done in time.'* ☐

I could fill many pages with what students have told me about exams and anxiety. But there is already quite a variety in the quotes above. They range from 'low-anxiety' (Students A and B) through to 'high-anxiety' (Students G and H), with a few moderately anxious students in between, and one (Student I) who claims to need the anxiety to get her working.

If you are anxious, I know there is no point telling you not to panic. That may make matters worse – it may make you anxious about being anxious.

But I will say this. Many students who say they are anxious actually do very well in examinations. Indeed, without a certain amount of anxiety, of working yourself up for a big occasion, you may not be able to rise to the mental and physical demands that examinations may make on you – especially if you have to take several within a few days. All the same, beyond a certain point, such pressure becomes unhealthy stress, and begins undermining your ability to do well.

Putting anxiety in its place

Sometimes students are right to feel anxious. They haven't worked as they should have on the course, and they hear the distant sound of chickens coming home to roost. But other students' anxiety is often less well founded. And facing up to it may enable them to do something to get rid of it or at least reduce it to productive proportions.

If you are at all anxious, is any of it due to:

1 Fears that examinations are designed specifically to reveal your hidden weaknesses? ☐

2 Uncertainty about what the examination will demand of you? ☐

3 Concern that your memory may not be up to it? ☐

4 Feelings that you have not mastered some of the important issues in the course? ☐

5 Doubts about your ability to think clearly enough under pressure and without access to texts, etc.? ☐

6 Lack of practice in sitting exams? ☐

7 Uncertainty as to how to prepare for exams? ☐

8 The sheer physical and mental exhaustion of 'living on your nerves' for weeks before the exam? ☐

9 Exam phobia (severe depression, paralysing panic, etc.)? ☐

Let's look at these anxieties one by one:

1 In most colleges your examiners will be your tutors – even if they have some guidance from external examiners. You have no reason to expect the Spanish Inquisition. No doubt there are exceptions, but most examiners (and I speak as one myself) take pains to design examinations in such a way as to enable you to reveal your abilities rather than your weaknesses. Apart from anything else, it casts doubt on the quality of our *teaching* if most students don't do at least reasonably well. Your failure could look like our failure.

   Nor shall we be subjecting your answers to endless nitpicking in the hope of finding footling errors we can deduct marks for. We'll be faced with dozens of scripts to mark in what seems like an impossibly brief period of time. We're not expecting flawless answers – few people can do their best work in examination conditions. Just give us some reasonably coherent and structured answers to the questions we set (rather than the ones you *wish* we'd set), preferably in legible handwriting, and you'll speed up our task of finding good things we can reward you for.

2 There is no need to be so uncertain about what the examination will demand of you that it makes you anxious. I've said something about this in Chapter 3 (pages 44–52) and we'll look at it again in this chapter. The key to dealing with this anxiety is *preparation*.

3 Most college examinations do not reward memory so much as evidence of understanding and the ability to think, argue a case or solve problems. In fact, if you read what examiners write about the papers they've marked, you'd get the impression that candidates often rely *too much* on memory and too little on selecting from what they know and using it intelligently. Typical examiners' reports say:

   'Too many answers are crammed with regurgitated detail that is either irrelevant or whose relevance is not made clear'; and

   'Candidates . . . spill out all they know on the topic, almost completely omitting to address themselves in any critical way to the *question* in which these terms appear.'

   Clearly, you *do* have to remember things to succeed in exams – just as you have to remember things to cope with everyday life.

But one of the themes of this book is that memory (of the sort you'll mostly need in college exams) is developed by making sense of ideas, finding meaning in them, understanding them – and by making fairly frequent use of them. If there *are* facts and figures that you do need consciously to memorize, then there are many books describing suitable memory joggers (mnemonics).

4 You certainly won't have mastered all of the important issues in the course. But nor will most of your colleagues. It is very easy to be so impressed by the issues other students are on top of (as was student E) that you forget that you have mastered topics *they* have not. Different students will get different things out of the course, and it would be an unusual exam that required you to have mastered everything in a course.

7 Any anxieties in these areas can be greatly eased by appropriate practice in exam techniques over the period in which you are preparing for the exams. We'll be looking at how to get such practice later in this chapter.

8 Many people do get themselves so worked up and tense during the weeks before exams that they find it difficult either to concentrate or to relax. Daily physical exercise – jogging, walking, swimming, whatever is convenient – can be very relaxing. So, of course, can the kind of relaxation technique suggested in Chapter 4 – especially if you've already got the habit well established before you start to feel under real pressure. However, if you are so tense or anxious that it is interfering with your ability to do a good job, discuss it with your doctor as soon as possible.

9 If, by any misfortune, you are one of these very few students who experience extreme and unmanageable symptoms at the prospect of examinations, see your doctor right away. With your doctor's backing, you should find that your college will have a way of dealing with you sympathetically.

When students fail to do themselves justice in an exam it is usually because of faults in their preparation for exams and/or in their examination technique. Preparation and technique is what we'll concentrate on in the rest of this chapter.

Preparing for examinations

Suppose you've got an important examination six months from now. How long before the exam would you think it sensible to start preparing?

Perhaps that was rather a vague question and you'd be justified in saying: 'It all depends what you mean by "preparing".' I would say you begin preparing the moment you start seriously and systematically applying your mind to understanding the issues in your course. I don't mean understanding the issues with a view to satisfying examiners, but with a view to satisfying yourself.

You will lay the foundations for exam success by studying reflectively and realistically throughout the period of the course – drawing where appropriate on the kinds of idea discussed in earlier chapters of this book. Such thoughtful studying will enable you to understand more, remember better and be more skilled in organizing your ideas quickly and effectively.

I think there are two chief elements in preparing for exams:

1 Revising.

2 Practising doing what the exam requires of you.

The role of revision

The key role in preparing for exams is played by revision. Literally, this means 'to see again'. Few of us can grasp a complex issue, and all its applications and ramifications, just from one encounter. We need to 'see it again' – preferably from different angles and in different contexts – before it really becomes embedded in our way of looking at the world.

So, to sharpen up on my previous question: How soon do you think you ought to start revising?

Again, you may have good grounds for feeling otherwise, but I would say that, in one sense, the answer should be now. To get inside your subject, revision should be a regular part of your learning habits right from the beginning of your course. With some short (e.g. 10-week courses) this is vital if you are to be ready for the end-of-course exam.

Revision as part of learning

Week after week, new ideas will be flying in at you, battling for a place alongside other recently acquired ideas – and many of them trying to displace common sense ideas that have suited you well for so long and which your mind may be reluctant to part with. The only way to cope with this onslaught is to keep looking back over the main ideas and issues you have already confronted. Keep 'seeing them again' by refreshing your memory about them and checking how well they stand up in the light of your more recent learning and experience.

Let me make one thing clear. Although we are here considering revision in the context of examination preparation, some such approach would be essential in mastering any complex subject over a period of time – *regardless* of whether or not you face an exam at the end. In other words, you are revising in order to *learn* – not just in order to perform well in an exam.

However, taking both purposes together, there are two very good reasons for doing regular revision right from the start. For one thing, you might not have time to revise everything you felt you needed to if you left it all until just before an exam. Second, and more important from the learning point of view, early and continuous revising will make the later material *easier to learn*. You will have a deeper understanding of what precedes it; and the more you have learned, the easier it is to learn related material.

An essential element in revision, whether or not you face an exam, is *reflection*. Think back over the course so far, try to recall the main ideas and issues, and consider whether you are more hazy about some than others and what you might need to do about this.

How much time (say, per week) might you think it reasonable to devote to this sort of revision in the *early stages* of your course?

Well, it's your decision, but you might start with about one hour per week thinking back over what you have learned (or failed to learn to your satisfaction) so far. It might be helpful to schedule this 'reflection hour' for a particular time every week – say, Friday afternoon or Sunday evening.

A revision timetable

As the course proceeds, you may find it worthwhile to increase the time you spend on this reflective revision. (Beware the revision advice in some 'how to study' books, for if you follow it you'll soon find yourself spending so much time revising the ever-growing amount you've learned already that there's no time left for learning anything new!)

When the examination is drawing near, you may need to spend practically all your study time on revision. For the final month or two you may want to work out a revision timetable. That is:

● Make a list of the topics you plan to revise

● Decide what order you want to tackle them in

● Space out the revision for each topic and make a note of which aspects of it you intend to work on during each week or day of your revision period

● Consider whether you might usefully plan to revise more than one topic each day (to ensure variety and interest)

● But leave plenty of time for rest and recreation – especially in the last few days before the exam

Revising with colleagues

A recurring theme of this book has been that you might benefit from collaboration with other students in some sort of 'self-help' study group. Not only might you all gain by comparing your general approaches to learning and studying, but you might also usefully share your insights on particular assignments or study tasks. Clearly, one such very important study task is revision.

So, even if you haven't yet formed your own self-help group, now might be a very good time to get together with two or three fellow-students to form a 'revision syndicate'. The idea would be to meet *regularly* – perhaps a couple of times a week for an hour or two – and revise topics *together*.

For instance, thinking of the colleagues you might work with in syndicate, which of the following benefits might you expect?

● A wider sense of what the main issues in the course are ☐

● More knowledge of 'cues' or hints as to which topics are most and least likely to be tested in the exam ☐

● Group brainstorming of approaches to an exam question ☐

- A chance to strengthen my own learning by 'teaching' my colleagues some aspect or topic I have understood more deeply than they have, or by learning from them ☐

- Discussion of assignments that members of the group have had marked and commented on during the course ☐

- Mutual commenting on one another's draft answers to questions from past examination papers ☐

- Arranging 'mock exams' together and critiquing one another's answers ☐

- An incentive to keep up the momentum on revision ☐

- The psychological support that might help me keep the exams in proportion and minimize anxiety ☐

How to revise

One of the first things to decide, either alone or in discussion with colleagues, is *which topics to revise*. You will not have time to revise everything in the course, even if you wish you could. But, in any case, you will probably be sufficiently 'cue-conscious' (see Chapter 3) to exclude some topics as either:

(a) unlikely to come up

(b) difficult for you to do well on even if they did

If you are a 'cue-seeker', you may want to be highly selective in which topics you tackle and which you leave alone. There are considerable dangers in this, however, unless you have reliable inside information as to what is going to come up in the exam. A rough rule of thumb you may find useful is to let the number of topics you revise be *twice* the number of questions you will be expected to answer. Applying such a rule depends, of course, on your understanding of past examination papers.

Analysing past exam papers

Get together a set of past exam papers in your subject and analyse them. If you can do this in company with fellow-students, so much the better. But do it. Analyse them from the point of (a) structure and (b) content (topics covered/kinds of answer expected). All except the last three questions below are concerned with structure.

For example, which of these questions can you *already* answer about each examination you will be taking?

- How long does the examination last? ☐
- Shall I be given any advance notice of the topics or questions? ☐
- What books and/or other materials am I allowed to take into the examination room? ☐
- How many questions shall I have to answer? ☐
- Do questions sometimes contain options within them? ☐
- Are some questions likely to be compulsory? ☐
- Is the exam paper divided into parts, with a requirement that I answer one or more questions from certain parts? ☐
- If so, what is the difference between the questions in the different parts? ☐
- Do some questions carry more marks than others? ☐
- Which topics have appeared with greatest frequency over the last three years or so? ☐
- Have any topics on which considerable stress has been put in my course (perhaps very up-to-date topics) not yet been asked about in past exams? ☐
- What do the questions ask me to *do* with the topics – e.g. describe, analyse, calculate, explain, criticize, evaluate, argue a point of view, or what? (See the glossary of verbs at the end of Chapter 10.) ☐

Knowing the answer to such questions as these should help focus your revision. That is, **you should be able to practise doing what the examination will require you to do.** *It should therefore also help you get started all the faster and more confidently on the day they put the real examination paper in front of you.*

Active revising

Although revision means 'seeing again', you might do well to think of it as 'seeing again but *differently*'. For instance, you'd get little value out of merely rereading stuff you've read before. First, the examination will require you to *recall* what you have learned. The fact that you can recognize ideas when you read them again is no guarantee that you'd recall them in an exam. Therefore, when you come to read your notes and essays again (and maybe check other texts), do so only *after* having tried to recall the main ideas they contain.

Second, the examination is unlikely to require you to display your ideas in the form you first met them. It won't be testing whether you've managed to get pages of print into your head. It will be concerned, instead, with whether you can make use of the ideas those pages contained and argue around the issues involved. That is to say, you are likely to be expected to set out the ideas *in your own words*, to *combine* them again and to use them in *new ways*.

In trying to get new viewpoints on topics, *force* yourself to view them differently. In working through your old notes and essays, be *critical*. Perhaps you won't find this too difficult. After all, you are now older than when you first wrote them. Do they now seem at all unclear, ignorant, muddled, misguided, arrogant, simplistic, one-sided – embarrassing?

Try to uncover the weaknesses. Hunt out your omissions and faults of emphasis. Assault your notes and essays with the newer insights and more mature viewpoints you will have gained since you first wrote them. (Do the comments your tutors wrote on your essays at the time make any more sense to you now?) Use your old material as an opportunity to test out your newer understandings.

Then rewrite your notes ruthlessly. Above all, *condense* them. Write brief summaries and outlines that contain the essential ideas and vital details. For instance, you may be able to reduce your notes and an essay on a topic to a single side of paper on which you've jotted all the *key words and phrases* that are sufficient to bring the whole lot back to mind.

So much for restructuring your knowledge. This we all need to do regularly throughout life, anyway, if we are to keep alive mentally. But you have a more immediate purpose for doing so. You are soon to sit an examination. To many students, this seems like an unnatural act; it certainly is a special one. So it is worth *training* for specially.

Training yourself for the examination

On the day you walk into the examination room, you will feel more relaxed, more confident and more competent if you've been through something like it many times before. (If you are doing a series of short courses, you probably will have been!)

A five-stage approach

What you might like to consider, as part of your preparation, is an approach that could both increase your competence and reduce whatever anxiety you may be feeling. This approach is a bit like the treatment used in dealing with phobias – 'progressive desensitization' (or 'getting used to it bit by bit').

The five stages of this approach are as follows:

1 Analyse past examination papers

2 Choose questions and plan answers in *outline* form (without referring to notes or other materials)

3 Outline and then write *complete* answers

4 Write complete answers within the *time limit* you would expect to have for each answer within the exam

5 Sit complete *mock exams* under conditions as much like the real thing as you can manufacture

You may need quite a bit of practice at one stage before moving on to the next. You will also want to go back from a stage you've reached in order to get more practice at a previous stage.

If you are working in a revision syndicate, your colleagues should be able to give you helpful feedback. Failing that, can you ask a tutor (if necessary, your personal tutor) to comment on some practice exam answers? At the very least, consider asking a friend or partner; they may be able to make thought-provoking comments even if they know little or nothing of the subject of your course.

Let me amplify the five-stage approach I've outlined above.

Analysing an examination paper

You may have started this already. You may have noticed the 'structural' points we discussed earlier. You may also have collected questions together and grouped them according to topic.

At the very least, you should make sure what is expected of you. After many examinations, the examiners produce a report on the strengths and weaknesses displayed by candidates in general. These may not be available to you in your college but, whether they are or not, most such reports are full of remarks like these:

- 'Many students clearly haven't read the instructions. They fail to notice that they are expected to answer at least one question from each section. Again, they omit to answer some parts of a multi-part question or, conversely, they answer *both* parts of an either/or question.'

- 'Students ignore or misinterpret the verb that tells them what to do with the subject of the question. This, unfortunately, seems particularly common with those who have a "prepared" answer they wish to regurgitate.'

- 'Students often misread (whether deliberately or not) the subject matter being asked about and write, for example, of micro-economic analysis when they were asked to discuss macro-economic analysis.'

- 'The weaker candidates show no signs of having planned an answer but leap about from point to point, and even if conclusions are arrived at, they tend to be stated baldly (almost as an afterthought) rather than being led up to through logical argument and effective use of evidence.'

- 'Too many answers are a bewildering and irritating tangle of bumptious value judgements, woolly theorizing and wild generalizations based on personal experiences that are far from typical.'

- 'Why are there always some candidates who have no sense of time? It is tragic when the candidate has written three good answers but has had no time to do more than scribble a paragraph or two on the final question. Candidates need reminding that three answers cannot be relied on to produce as good a result as they'd get by tackling all four.'

Which of the above errors do you feel you may have committed in the past?

Most of us, I think, will admit to one or more of the errors. As far as we were concerned, of course, they may have been not so much errors as attempts to con the examiners. As you see, such attempts can be sadly counter-productive!

Outlining answers

Don't just browse through your old exam papers telling yourself:

'Yes, I could manage numbers 1, 4 and 7, but I would be in trouble with 2, 3 and 8, and I can't imagine what 6, 9 and 10 are on about.'

You can't be sure of how you'd really manage until you actually practise answering such questions.

One of the most useful ways of giving yourself practice is to write answers in *outline* form. Begin by weighing up the question and deciding what it is asking for:

(a) Make sure you know what *subject matter* it is referring to

(b) *Underline* the key verb that tells you what to do (or if none is explicitly stated, decide what is implied – see the glossary on pages 205–208)

Jot down the main ideas and supporting detail you would want to bring into your answer. Then write down the key steps of your argument as a skeleton outline, just as you would before writing a normal essay.

If you are in a revision syndicate you should be able to give one another valuable feedback on your outline answers. It could be useful for all members of the syndicate to outline an answer to the *same* question. Comparison of your different approaches could be very instructive. Another variation would be for the group to choose half a dozen questions on a common topic (perhaps including some that members of the group have made up), revise that topic and then allocate a question at random for each member of the group to answer.

Since planning is the most crucial step in answering a question, you may want to spend most of your training time writing outlines. After all, you can plan two or three answers in the time it would take you to plan and write out the complete answer for just one question.

Writing complete answers

There is a difference between planning and writing, however. A good out-line in note form is no guarantee that you will be able to turn it into flowing prose. So you need to practise writing some complete answers. If possible, get colleagues to read and discuss them, and do the same for theirs. You should be able to get almost as much out of reading and com-menting on other students' work as you get from hearing what they have to say about yours. It should clarify not only your views of the subject matter but also help you to understand better the kind of criteria exam-iners are likely to use in appraising your work.

As a step towards realistic exam conditions try answering a question from two or three chosen for you by a colleague.

Writing to time limits

This is the next and crucial step towards practising what the exam requires of you. Don't just plan and write your answer, but do so within the time you'd be able to allow yourself for this under real exam condi-tions. Again, if possible, get your colleagues to help by presenting you with a limited list of questions to choose from. (If you have to answer, say, four out of twelve in the exam, then they might give you three from which to choose your one.) Also, if two or three of you can sit down together to work to the time limit, you will be able to make sure no one overruns and also get practice in thinking and writing in the presence of others doing likewise (as you will in the exam room).

Apart from everything else, this is an opportunity to knock your hand-writing into examination form – reasonably speedy but still sufficiently legible. Get your colleagues to tell you if some of your words are difficult to read.

Sitting mock exams

The aim here is to create something as much like exam conditions as you can get. Take an exam paper you have not looked at before. (It could be one you have helped compile with colleagues, provided you purposely ignore any question you have contributed yourself.) Then sit down, preferably with colleagues similarly engaged, and spend three hours (or whatever is normally allowed) producing the best answers you can. For some thoughts about how to do this, see what I have to say under the heading 'In the examination room' in a few pages' time.

Follow your examination session, after a decent 'recovery time', by assessing and discussing one another's answers.

You probably won't have time to give yourself too many mocks, but if you have any doubts about your ability to work flat out during the hours of an exam, they can be an excellent way of breaking yourself in. At least you shouldn't expire from shock when you finally do face the real thing.

Keep all your practice work, whether outline notes or full answers. They could be particularly valuable for last-minute revision of vital topics. You may also want to exchange photocopies of some materials with colleagues.

Which of the five stages of training yourself for the exam do you think you would want to spend *most* (+) and which *least* (–) time on altogether?

1 Analysing past exam papers ☐

2 Outlining answers ☐

3 Writing complete answers ☐

4 Answering to a time limit ☐

5 Sitting complete mock exams ☐

Only you can decide what might best suit your needs. Personally, I'd want to find time for two or three mocks, especially if I was facing several exams and hadn't sat any for some time. But I'd no doubt spend a much larger proportion of my total preparation time writing outlines and timed answers.

To sum up, then: successful revision needs to be started early. Only brief sessions at first, perhaps, but with more and more of your time being devoted to it as exams draw nearer. You need to find out all you can about the exam and practise doing the things you will have to do in the examination room. And you may well find benefits in working as a member of a revision syndicate.

As you near the end of your revision period, ask yourself: 'What have I learned about *myself* – my strengths and weaknesses and special interests – that I might be able to use in the examination?'

Your final day

All too soon, perhaps, you will find your revision timetable has been eaten away. You have reached the day before your examination. If you have more than one examination then, of course, you may have several of these 'final days'.

How to spend it?

Students spend this final day in a variety of ways according to temperament and how exhausted or hyped-up they feel. How do you think you will want to spend it?

- Switch off all conscious thought of the examination, do no work at all, and go out walking, running, playing some sport or whatever helps you relax ☐

- Continue with normal revision, carrying on with exactly the same routine as you've followed for the last few days/ weeks ☐

- Make a last-minute attempt to catch up on areas of the curriculum that you feel you may have neglected so far ☐

The important thing here is to do what you feel you want to do, ignoring what other people say you should be doing or what they say they are doing. However, if you do spend your final day revising (or even trying to get on top of material you should have learned long ago), do try to break off at least two hours before bedtime to ensure your mind winds down sufficiently to allow you to sleep.

Try reading something entertaining, watching television or nattering with any friends who are not obsessed with examinations. Go to bed early enough to get at least as much sleep as you normally need. Remember that, next day, a fresh alert mind will be far more useful to you than a few more facts packed in behind the sickening headache and general doziness you gained from sitting up all night.

There is one thing you can profitably do on the evening before your exam. That is to make sure you have all the equipment you'll need next day: plenty of pens (and ink, if necessary), pencils, ruler, watch, mathematical instruments, calculator – whatever is likely to be useful for the paper you'll be taking.

Oh, and pardon me for mentioning it (but there's always someone who gets it wrong) – do check that you'll be turning up for the right exam at the right place at the right time on the right day!

On your way to the exam

If you can, avoid doing a 'preview' on the way to the exam. Especially avoid talking about the prospects with other students. It's so easy to get depressed and alarmed at the thought of all the topics you might have paid attention to and haven't. Keep to yourself, and remain confident that you have done everything it was in your power to do. Even if you haven't, worrying now will only make matters worse. If you must think about the forthcoming paper, let your thoughts be *positive* and *specific*. Concentrate on just one possible question and organize an outline answer in your mind.

In the examination room

So at last the moment arrives. You are in the examination room. You may be tense, keyed-up to meet the challenge, but I trust you are not in fear and trembling. After all, you have trained yourself for this moment – you have been through something very similar several times before. You are *prepared*. While you are waiting for the 'off', you may find it helpful to do slow, deep breathing or practise some other relaxation technique (see page 61).

When 'zero hour' arrives, the invigilator will say something like: 'You may now open your question paper and begin.' What is likely to be your first reaction?

- To hunt for a question that looks 'do-able' and start writing out my first answer ☐

- To read every question very carefully before I write a word ☐

- To read the instructions about how candidates are expected to tackle the paper ☐

I hope your first reaction will be to read very carefully through the whole paper – including the instructions. Too many students blow their chances by hunting frantically for the first question that looks vaguely familiar – or mentions some subject matter they happen to have prepared an answer to – and plunge straight into an answer without so much as a glance at the other questions or the instructions to candidates.

Check the instructions

Before you do anything else, read the instructions. These will usually be at the beginning of the paper, but there may be additional ones later at the start of any sections. How long have you got for the paper? How many questions do you have to answer? Are any of them compulsory? Do some questions carry more marks than others? Is the paper divided into two or more sections, with so many questions to be answered from each? Does each answer have to be started on a new sheet of paper? And so on.

You'll probably know most of these answers from your practice with previous papers – but it pays to check, for the rules may have changed. Every examination brings its rueful crop of students who've wasted weeks of conscientious learning and revision by answering four questions instead of three, or who didn't notice they had to answer all the questions in section A, or who thought they had three hours, not two and a half, for the paper.

Read all the questions

Then pay individual attention to each and every question. Make sure you know what each question is asking for, and what it is *not* asking for. Be cool and objective, and don't misread the questions. Don't try, as many students do, to twist them into the questions you *wish* had been asked instead. Just remember the theological student who, when asked to evaluate the relative contributions of Jewish and Greek ideas to the development of Christianity, is said to have written, modestly: 'Far be it from me to offer judgements on an issue about which the leading authorities cannot agree. Instead, I hereby append a list of the twelve tribes of Israel'!

Pay particular attention to the verbs or phrases that tell you what you are supposed to *do* in your answers. It's a good idea to *underline* them. Needless to say, if you 'describe' when you are asked to 'analyse', or if you 'account for' instead of 'evaluate', you will have failed to answer the question. And you're unlikely to get much credit if you simply 'write around' the subject.

You may get some questions in which no verb or phrase is stated explicitly, e.g.

a) 'Did the modern concept of . . .?'

b) 'What effects did . . .?'

c) 'Is it the case that . . .?'

In such cases, you will have to decide for yourself what is the verb or 'action phrase' that lies behind the question.

Looking back at the glossary on pages 205–208, select one or two verbs or phrases that might indicate what each of these three is wanting you to do.

With (a) the implied verb or phrase might be, for example, 'evaluate' or 'to what extent?'; with (b) it might perhaps be 'describe' or 'explain'; and with (c) it might be 'criticize' or 'argue'. It is impossible to be more certain without seeing the rest of the questions – and even then you may have to make an inspired guess, based on what you judge to be the examiners' general expectations of students working at your level.

As you read through the questions, trying to work out what the examiners are after, put a mark against those you feel you might be able to answer. In deciding which questions are 'possibles', remember to play to your strengths. Remember what you've learned about yourself – your strengths and weaknesses, and special interests – during your revision period. Look for questions that will allow you to show your own personal flair. But, at the same time, don't get out of your depth by taking on a question that's too tough for you. Be realistic. There are no special marks for bravery beyond the call of realism.

Decide your writing order

Having chosen your questions, in what order are you going to answer them? This is usually up to you. But if there is a compulsory question you may decide to tackle it first in order to ensure it doesn't get neglected if, by any chance, you start tiring later. Otherwise, you may think it a good idea to start with your 'best' question, so that you can really get into your stride with something you feel confident about.

Budget your time

The next major step – and, yes, you possibly haven't written a word yet – is to write down your *target finishing time* for each answer. In order to do this, you must first decide how long you can spend on each question. The best plan is usually to allocate your time according to the number of marks allowed for each answer. If, so far as you can tell, all carry equal marks, then you divide your time among them equally.

So you have, let's say, four questions to answer in three hours. How long per question? Not forty-five minutes, for you'll have used up five to ten minutes by the time you are ready to start planning your first answer, and you should allow yourself another ten to fifteen minutes at the end for a final check-up on all answers. So you may decide you have forty minutes or less to spend on each question. (If the structure of the paper is the same as on previous occasions, and you have been practising with such papers, then you will presumably have thought all this through before.) But look at the clock now, do the necessary calculations and write down your expected finishing time for each answer.

Plan your answers

Before you begin to write each answer, you should prepare some sort of skeleton outline (see Chapter 9). In the exam situation, such an outline can give you even more help than usual in keeping a firm control over your writing. It should ensure you produce a well-ordered statement or logical argument rather than a ragbag of jumbled outpourings. Besides, students who've run out of time in an examination have often been awarded almost as many marks for submitting a clear outline as they would have got for a complete essay.

So, reread each question you are going to tackle, perhaps ringing words you think are essential cues to what the question is getting at. Jot down all the main ideas and possibly useful details that occur to you. Do a bit of brainstorming and just let the points come into your mind as they will. Not all will be equally useful, but scribble them down anyway. Then select the main ideas you are going to put across, and work out the most sensible sequence in which to present them. Write an outline of your answer in whatever form you normally do this. Be brutal with yourself in keeping out any material which (however painstakingly you've learned it) is irrelevant to the question as asked. You might reasonably spend up to a quarter of your total answer time, and sometimes more, on this planning and outlining.

Furthermore, some students would recommend that you outline *every* answer before you write out any one of them in full. How do you feel about this suggestion?

You know your own circumstances and your own temperament best. I know that planning all answers first does not suit everybody. But the three benefits claimed for it are these:

1 You can more easily treat your answers as a set that will show to advantage the range of your knowledge and competencies. You are giving your unconscious mind a chance to work for you.

2 Having planned out all the answers, your unconscious mind is likely to continue working away at the task even while you are writing your first answer. So, by the time you come to write the later ones, you may find you see some fresh ways of improving on your original plan. (This may be another good reason for leaving your weaker questions until last.)

3 Once you've completed your preliminary planning of all answers, you have the comfort of knowing exactly what ground you've got to cover in the remaining time. You have only to expand on your outlines.

It takes nerve to spend perhaps the first hour writing a complete set of detailed outlines – especially if everyone else around you is clearly writing full answers. I leave you to decide whether or not it might suit your style. Might it be worth trying out in one of your own mocks?

Write your answers

The style of your written answers should be the same as that of other essays you write – simple, direct and to the point. Even if you are asked to write 'notes' or 'short answers', write in complete sentences and give each answer a clear beginning, middle and end. Pay attention to spelling and grammar. Be particularly careful not to misspell words that appear on the question paper.

Make your writing as *legible* as possible. Think of your examiner who has to deal with dozens of such scripts. He or she is likely to be less than sympathetic if the logic of your line of argument is lost in an untidy scrawl of handwriting.

Keep your mind on one question at a time while you are writing. But be prepared to jot down any ideas that may suddenly occur to you for use in other answers.

Watch the clock

Stick firmly to the finishing times you have set yourself. If you run out of time on a particular question (or if you get bogged down in it), *stop* writing. Leave a big space on your answer sheet in case you can come back to finish off later, but get right on with the next question.

If you are *sure* that just another couple of minutes would enable you to round off your answer more satisfactorily, then you might allow yourself a little extra time. But be warned. Many students come to grief because they spend too long on their best questions.

Whatever happens, don't omit your final answer. Making some sort of stab at the final question will probably earn you more marks than trying to improve one of your earlier ones. It should take you less trouble to get from zero per cent (the mark for an unanswered question) to, say, twenty-five per cent (for a partially answered one) than to improve an essay from, say, sixty per cent to eighty-four per cent.

At the very least, give in your skeleton outline to show the examiners what form your argument would have taken in answering that final question. If, by any chance, you didn't even write a skeleton outline, jot down a few notes now and submit them. Anything might win you a few extra marks at this point. Nothing can do you more harm than simply ignoring the final question.

Check everything

If you have managed to stick to your finishing times, you should have a few minutes in hand when you have completed your last answer. Use them to make sure you've complied with all the instructions. Have you numbered your answers? Crossed out rough notes that you want the examiner to ignore? Put your name or number on whatever you are handing in? And so on.

Ideally, you should also have enough time (five to ten minutes can make all the difference) for a final scan through what you've written. Look out for:

- slips of the pen – e.g. 'causal relationships' written as 'casual relationships' throughout

- slips of the mind that too easily occur under examination pressure – e.g. a vital 'not' left out of a sentence

- clumsy expressions

- faulty spelling or grammar

- miscalculations in numerical answers

- unlabelled or misdrawn graphs

- illegible phrases that can be rewritten

Such a final check is never a waste of time. It is simply a professional way to finish off the job. Many students pick up five to ten per cent of their total marks in this last round-up. Besides, it is better to have a last-minute inspiration while checking through your paper than while going home on the bus.

After the examination

Once you've handed in your answers, don't hang around for those depressing post-mortems with other students. They rarely make you happy about the good things you have written, and too often leave you brooding about the things you've left unsaid. You've done your best, and no single person could include all the points that everyone else happens to have thought of. So try to forget all thoughts of how you might have done better.

Such thoughts are particularly unsettling if you have another examination looming up. So get right away, enjoy as much recreation as you can allow yourself, and then resume training for your next bout with the examiner.

Learn from the experience

However, once the examination is well behind you – perhaps after you've heard the result – you may think the experience is worth reflecting on. Think about the strategy you adopted – from beginning your revision to checking your final answer. How realistic was your approach? What were its strong points? What were its weaknesses? What would you do again? What would you avoid? What would you change? How might you do things differently next time you find yourself being examined – whether in college or not, and whether in a written examination or some other kind of test?

How much you can learn from your experience depends to a large extent on how much feedback you get from the examiners. Colleges differ in this.

For example, which of the following happens in your college – (a) for exams *during* your programme of studies and (b) for exams (finals?) at the *end* of the programme?

	During	End
● We get told only whether we have passed or failed overall	☐	☐
● We get told whether we have passed or failed on each paper	☐	☐
● We get told marks/grades/percentages (but no comments from examiners) on the exams as a whole	☐	☐
● We get marks, etc. (but no comments) on each paper	☐	☐
● We get comments but no marks, etc.	☐	☐
● We get our examination answers returned	☐	☐
● We have class discussions about the issues tested in the exam and how we handled them	☐	☐

Obviously, the more information you get back from your examiners, the more you can learn:

a) about your understanding of the subject matter of the exam

b) about how you approached this particular exam

c) how you might best approach future courses and future exams

As I say, colleges differ in how much information they give. I hope your college is more communicative than one of Britain's largest universities where, until recently at least, tutors were forbidden to tell students which of the different subjects of the Part I examinations they'd done best in – at the very time when they were supposed to be deciding which of these subjects to specialize in for Part II.

If you do get your answers returned, analyse them against the original questions, and consider the examiner's grading and/or comments. If possible, compare your answers with those of other students, and ask your tutors for further comment. What were your strengths and weaknesses? Where did you lose credit? Did you misinterpret any questions? Did you leave out any important ideas or vital detail? Were any answers illogical or poorly argued? Did you misunderstand any key ideas in the course? How would you write the answer if such a question were to come up again? How might you avoid having similar trouble with questions in the future? By analysing any mistakes in this way, you may be able to identify both better ways of learning and better ways of tackling examinations.

And if, by chance, you are disappointed with your performance, don't let it make you feel bad about yourself as a person or even as a learner. Exams are a lottery. How well you do depends not just on your knowledge and understanding and your powers of expression. It also depends on what questions happen to come up and whether you've got examiners who are sympathetic or unsympathetic to your approach. As one tutor–examiner told me recently:

> *'It's just too painful and embarrassing to admit how much we differ in our marking. I've tried to open up discussion about the criteria we are using but this is seen as disruptive. So we just keep on doing it, because we can't see any better way.'*

Next time you'll get a different set of questions and maybe a different set of examiners. Perhaps they'll be more on your wavelength. In the meantime, don't think about them – just concentrate on getting all you can out of your course.

> **If you've done reasonably well on your assignments during a course, you are entitled to expect an examination that enables you to do reasonably well at the end of it.**

Follow-up activities

1 Try to find out as much as you can about how the examination system works in your college – both the official version and the 'hidden curriculum' version. The latter you may be able to learn about in discussion with students who've been through the course ahead of you. Regard all sources of information with caution and be prepared to form your own judgement as to what really goes on.

2 Consider forming a revision syndicate – based perhaps on your self-help group if you already have one.

3 Collect past examination papers, and examiners' reports if there are any to be had.

4 Ask your tutor(s), with support from colleagues if possible, for a discussion on examinations and the kinds of faults that students on your kind of course are liable to make.

5 Aim to enjoy your course – in spite of exams.

References

In case you can spare a little more time from your studies to read about studying and learning, here are some references to material that may interest you. You will notice that I have included both printed and online resources.

Books about learning

The following books are written primarily for college teachers, but all take the student's experience of learning as the focus of attention. My guess is that you would find most of them more illuminating than the majority of how-to-study books. These books are based on research into how students actually do study and learn – not on someone's opinions about how they 'ought' to study and learn. You may feel like mentioning some of them to your teachers! I would especially recommend the Marton book – a collection of articles representing most of the areas of research into student learning (and well illustrated by case studies and the recorded comments of students). But browsing and grazing in any of these books may give you a refreshing new slant on the business of studying. In particular, they may help you see more clearly what your tutors may be expecting of you and what, in turn, you might expect from them (see Chapter 3).

Beard, R.M. and Senior, I.J., *Motivating Students*, Routledge & Kegan Paul, London, 1980.

Boud, D., *et al.*, *Reflection: Turning Experience into Learning*, Kogan Page, London, 1985.

Gibbs, G., *Learning by Doing: A Guide to Teaching and Learning Methods*, FEU, London, 1988.

——, *Teaching Students to Learn: A Student-Centred Approach*, Open University Press, Milton Keynes, 1981.

Honey, P. & Mumford, A., *The Manual of Learning Styles*, available direct from Dr Peter Honey, 10 Linden Avenue, Maidenhead, Berks SL6 6HB, 1986, (*Activists, theorists, etc*) (See page 29.)

Hudson, L., *Frames of Mind*, Methuen, London, 1968. (*Syllbs and Syllfs*) (See page 27.)

Marton, F., *et al.*, *The Experience of Learning*, Scottish Academic Press, Edinburgh, 1984. (*Surface/deep level* and many other aspects of learning) (See page 23.)

Miller, C.M.L. and Parlett, M., *Up to the Mark: A Study of the Examination Game*, SRHE, Guildford, 1974. (*Cue-consciousness*) (See page 50.)

Morgan, A., *Improving Your Students' Learning*, Kogan Page, London, 1993.

Perry, W.G., *Forms of Intellectual and Ethical Development in the College Years: A Scheme*, Holt, Rinehart & Winston, New York, 1970. (See page 32.)

Ramsden, P. (ed.), *Improving Learning: New Perspectives*, Routledge, London, 1992.

Rogers, C., *Freedom to Learn*, Merril, Columbus (Ohio), 1969.

Rowntree, D., *Developing Courses for Students*, Harper & Row, London, 1985.

——, *Assessing Students: How Shall We Know Them*, Kogan Page, London, 1987.

Schmeck, R. (ed.), *Learning Strategies and Learning Styles*, Plenum Press, New York, 1988.

Snyder, B.R., *The Hidden Curriculum*, Knopf, New York, 1971. (See page 47.)

Some Internet sites

If you have access to the World Wide Web, you may also be interested in the following sites:

- *DeLiberations* – an electronic journal devoted to the improvement of teaching and learning in post-secondary education: http://www.lgu.ac.uk/deliberations/

- *Internet University* – a list of several hundred online college courses that you can take (for a fee) via the Internet: http://www.caso.com/iu/courses.html/

- *Journal of Interactive Media in Education* – a site where you can read

about and try out interactive computer-based learning media:
http://www-jime.open.ac.uk/jime/

- *Knowledge Media Institute* – for demonstrations and discussions of the Open University's use of computer-based learning media: http://kmi.open.ac.uk/

- *Mailbase* – a free service run from the University of Newcastle that enables you to discuss (or read how the experts discuss) many academic subjects online. For details of the subjects covered, consult:
http://www.mailbase.ac.uk/
or send the email message 'Send lists full' to
'mailbase@mailbase.ac.uk'

- *Spectrum Virtual University* – where you can sign up for a (free) online course delivered via the Web:
http://www.vu.org/

- *Tile.Net* – a gateway to free academic discussion lists like Mailbase, but chiefly in the USA and Canada:
http://tile.net/lists/

- *World Lecture Hall* – links to learning materials for a wide range of (chiefly on-campus) courses that have been made available online (often for free use by any students) by dozens of universities:
http://www.utexas.edu/world/lecture/

Index